IN PURSUIT OF
Happiness

Todd Saucier

INSPIRED BY A TRUE STORY

PAGE PUBLISHING
Conneaut Lake, PA

First originally published by Page Publishing 2022

ISBN 978-1-6624-8596-1 (pbk)
ISBN 978-1-6624-8586-2 (digital)

Printed in the United States of America

CONTENTS

When Born v

Introduction... vii

The Pursuit ix

Chapter 1: Innocence.. 1

Chapter 2: Divided 6

Chapter 3: Consequence 20

Chapter 4: Unexpectedly 36

Chapter 5: Magnificent.. 49

Chapter 6: Punishment 58

Chapter 7: Anticipating 70

Chapter 8: Interruption 85

Chapter 9: Embracing.. 97

Chapter 10: Wondering 103

Chapter 11: Difficulty 113

Chapter 12: Resolution... 131

Chapter 13: Survivor 138

Chapter 14: Inspiration...164

Chapter 15: Love's Greatest Challenge 175

WHEN BORN

When born we are unable to see.

Our lips without sound,

We float in warm water,

Our body is filled with innocence,

We lack worldly experiences,

Our body is unacquainted with hidden motive or intentions.

When born we begin learning the Do's and the Don'ts as the

dos bring the happiness and our feet share the excitement.

Our body continues to grow as we quickly learn how

we can get what we want or get what we need.

When delivered, we are out,

We are free,

We can barely see.

We cry and scream, as these are our words.

What do we want, or what do we need?

We learn and experience that both work well for attention, although

do they give us what we want or do they give us what we need?

INTRODUCTION

In our earliest days of life, as we grow as people, we begin to learn love as we feel the gentle touch of our mothers. Hope, courage, and happiness bloom like fresh flowers filled with soft petals and beautiful, brilliant colors, and we quickly learn how to be happy. Unknowingly, life's weeds and lack of water tend to make our branches harden and our colors and our petals weaken.

Our happiness becomes brittle and fear begins to blossom as it creeps within us, unknown and hidden.

As time changes, the dislikes and discomforts, little by little, emotionally, physically, and mentally, drain our relationships between family, friends, spouses, and partners.

Where the hope and love we are born with becomes challenged or forgotten. Interests of what we need seem suspended or impossible.

The mystery becomes the suspense as we grow as people. We quickly realize how to manipulate the outcome as we navigate through the pinhole of our journey, and it begins to be altered.

Suspense becomes the excitement, the path becomes covered by debris, and the inability to return or change back to the person that we were given in the beginning seems lost or unknown.

The kindness and love for others becomes challenged. Soon the judgments and mistreatments start to blossom as they are delivered to the unknown.

Life's unfairness takes hold. Its ugliness becomes known as it begins to be poured onto others. Our body language and words become ignored as they are spoken.

Is it possible the pursuit of happiness is to be challenged throughout life like our faith, where questions remain with lack of understanding, overfilling our cup as they spill out?

THE PURSUIT

This book was inspired by a true story. A young boy is injured at the age of eight and introduced to the first of many struggles, even today, with the aftereffects of a brain injury.

With the determination, love, and hope for himself, he fights for fairness where lack of judgment and mistreatment seem to go unchallenged, although consequences remain very real.

Through secrecy, maintaining concealment of his injury is unlikely. He does find happiness in small things each day. And he discovers tremendous love and joy inspiring others.

His story comes to you with love and hope and understanding. Life's moments survive in layers and sometimes still hold back the promise of happiness, love, and hope.

Surfaces become thin and the mounds of unhappiness steal the wealth of the beginning. Loneliness and fear become the lesson for tomorrow.

As a young boy, he began discovering life's greatest gifts, although challenged at a time when children lack the understanding of change and the intentions of others.

The time when excitement and adventure began to shape dreams. A single moment leads to lessons about love, happiness, hope, and dreams.

At times, his story will be disturbing, as the descriptions of events are real and contain actual scenes with content of verbal, emotional, physical, and sexual abuse.

CHAPTER 1

Innocence

The story begins on a cold winter day. It was January, and the ground crunched beneath your feet. The wind pressed against your face. The trace of rose-red cheeks became the reminder of human vulnerability. The year was 1960 when a father and mother of two would soon welcome the arrival of number three.

They lived in a small house in the city where white siding and black shutters cover its landscape, and many old cars fill its roadways.

In the early morning hours, when the light began to fill the window, a baby boy was born, and his name was Jimmy.

Jimmy had spent many days, and maybe a few nights, getting to know his brother and sister before he was even delivered into the world.

It was their touch, their voice, and laughter that communicated their love and happiness for him. At times it could be very loud, and others only a whisper.

Jimmy's sister was two years old, and his brother was four at the time, and they would soon see their baby brother for the first time.

It didn't take long for Jimmy to learn crying and screaming was not always going to get him the attention he wanted or needed. And by the look on his sister's face, the sounds were apparently disturbing.

As Jimmy rolled over and over, he soon discovered the comfort of rocking himself to sleep. It became habit as the last thing he would remember, until the sunlight in his window would deliver the new day.

The experience of throwing anything across the room seemed to only bring unwanted attention, and Jimmy avoided it as much as possible.

As the daily journey continued, Jimmy began learning about walking, running, talking, and adventure.

The discovery of accomplishments that seemed so challenging began to shape the very joy and happiness within him.

Jimmy had failed many times to accomplish his desire. Frustrated, disappointed, and sometimes even pained, Jimmy would try again. He realized he was actually becoming stronger. Failure became acceptable because the learning opportunity came with value.

Without knowing at the time, even with its disappointments and the frustration it brings, he found it part of life's journey. It was a benefit built in.

The part that most people wish didn't happen becomes the strengths for survival.

As Jimmy was running across the yard, he tripped and fell to the ground. The skin tore from his knee, and the wound began to bleed. Soon tears rolled from Jimmy's eyes.

"Can the leg continue to work with that big gash in my knee?" Jimmy asked. His mother quickly cleansed his wound and placed a small bandage on his scraped knee, and, without hesitation, Jimmy was running across the yard again.

"It's a miracle. My leg, it still works!"

The smile on Jimmy's face glowed with cheer. His recovery from his wound became the lesson. The fear of the unknown had become the victory of tomorrow. Around the same time, Jimmy had found one of the best parts of growing up was how good it felt not to have messy pants and that green slimy food in the jar.

Well, like most kids, it wasn't long before Jimmy was running the house for his mom and dad when the news of a new baby brother would make him a little less important.

Jimmy was extremely excited about having a baby brother, and moving from the city into a new house was icing on the cake.

It wasn't very clear what a little brother would be like, but with his brother and sister's excitement, it must be good.

Finally, the day that seemed so far away was before Jimmy's eyes. Within hours, he had a little baby brother, just four days before his second birthday.

It wasn't long before the discovery of horrifying crying and screaming filled Jimmy's ears. The new addition to the family became a seriously noticeable change.

He was perfect to Jimmy. He counted his little fingers and little toes. He cherished the fact he wouldn't have to change any of those diapers, because whatever comes out from babies not only looked like the food he used to eat, it smelled horrible.

Jimmy had very little idea what he had put his parents through when he was in diapers and now had a very clear understanding of the experience.

"I'm never having children."

When nap time came around for Jimmy's brother, he wasn't allowed in the room. Although when the crying and screaming remained his communication, he wanted to go in and tell him, "That's not going to work. You're on your own."

Although to Jimmy's surprise, his mother would go in and pick him up. Jimmy quickly asked himself, *Was I not crying and screaming loud enough? Were my words not clear? What was I doing wrong? I'll have to change my approach next time and see if it helps get me what I want.* It didn't help, although Jimmy thought, *I'm still the greatest thing that ever happened to this family. He's my little baby brother, and he needs more help than I do now that I'm two!*

CHAPTER 2

Divided

Meanwhile, Jimmy's family became very busy and seemed complete with his new little brother and their amazing new home. It had an incredibly big yard, and, to his surprise, a German shepherd puppy was also added to the family. He didn't stay small for long and barked way too much. Jimmy's mom was always getting complaints from the neighbors.

Suddenly, like a storm in the night, there were strong winds, hard rain, lighting, and thunder. Jimmy crawled from his bed to see what was happening.

As he walked around the corner of the kitchen, he found his dad pounding on the door, peering through the small picture-framed window in the porch door. His fear began to wonder.

When Jimmy's father noticed him standing there, he began asking Jimmy to open the door. The kitchen light had been turned on, and as he approached the door, his mother called out to Jimmy with the phone to her ear, telling him, "No, get away from the door, Jimmy."

The dog was barking, and his mother's voice was loud and angry. Jimmy stood rigid like his feet were glued to the floor. He looked back at the door only to find his father's face was no longer there. Jimmy's mother had hung up the phone and asked him to return to his room. He remained confused and worried for his dad, as an overwhelming fear took over every thought.

Jimmy had never heard his mother and father using these loud voices before. He looked around the room for his older brother or sister for any kind of answers. They were nowhere to be found.

Afraid and alone, with tears in his eyes, Jimmy lay in his bed. As the light appeared in his bedroom window and the sun began to shine in, Jimmy began to think over the night's confusing events.

The dog barking.

The pounding on the door.

The loud voices.

Where was his brother and sister?

Jimmy had so many questions without answers. So many worries with unknown consequences.

It was like a nightmare, when you wake up and realize you're in your bed and it wasn't real.

Why were you dreaming it?

What was its intention?

How can imagination appear so real?

Jimmy often wondered why dreams existed. Why can't they be filled with adventure and happiness? Instead, they are scattered stories, lacking any kind of happiness. It's like they are placed in a blender, and for the most part, fear is the only ingredient remembered.

Very little was said the next day, and it would be some time before Jimmy would see his father again. After a while, he would pick them up on the weekends. They would go to the movies and have popcorn and candy. This would bring Jimmy some happiness for just a short time. The tension and heartbreaking conversation seemed similar, where everyone was talking, although nothing was being said. The same thing over and over.

"It's nothing you need to worry about."

Jimmy was very young at the time, and, like many children, the thought of not all being together was awful and consumed his thoughts with disappointment.

Happiness seemed distant, or maybe not even an option.

His thought lacked understanding. Was his father not good to his mother, or was his mother not good to his father? It appeared like the secret grew between them as the days passed.

Jimmy knew very little about adult stuff. He often wondered if kid stuff was the problem. How could he or his brothers and sister make it better?

Later Jimmy learned his parents' disappointments with each other should maybe be kept private. They seemed to intentionally make them known as their imagination told them they each were the better person in the argument, making statements to each other they couldn't take back.

Jimmy felt at times kids are the forgotten ones after the storm. There are times parents would be looking for compassion for themselves, not realizing little people don't have any idea what's going on and exposing them to this behavior as acceptable.

Some time had passed and smoothed over many frustrations related to Jimmy's separated family. It seemed to present some happier days when they were able to spend time with either parent.

It was in the fall of 1964 when Jimmy would quickly learn about God-given fear for the first time.

Jimmy's older brother was burning leaves in the backyard, and Jimmy wanted to help.

The fire had been struggling a little and only burning around its edges. The day was warm and the sky was blue and the sun was shining like a bright light bulb right in their faces.

Jimmy had brought his brother a cup of water. He quickly swallowed the water and asked him to go to the garage and put a little gas in the Styrofoam cup.

Jimmy ran with excitement to the garage, put a little gas in the cup, when he quickly realized the cup was leaking. He began running back toward the fire.

With Jimmy's every step, it began leaking more and more. The bottom of the cup was disintegrating before his eyes. His hand was now covered with gas, and he began running across the yard as fast as possible before the cup would be empty.

Jimmy, without hesitation, threw the cup into the fire. The flames billowed into the sky as they followed the trail back to Jimmy's hand like a lightning bolt, and soon Jimmy was on fire.

To Jimmy's surprise, his big brother tackled him to the ground and started rolling him around until the fire was out.

He didn't realize at the time, but the pain of the burns and the tackle to the ground would be his first experience with appreciation for God's given fear for survival. They ran to the house for cool water for his badly burned hand before going to the hospital. Although

Jimmy ended up with second-degree burns to his hand and had the biggest blisters he had ever seen, he was blessed with a boxing glove bandage that made him look very cool.

It wasn't long before Jimmy was back playing and riding his bike. The fun became interesting when one of his blisters popped and his bright white bandage became yellow. After a few tears, Jimmy's bike was rolling again. He wasn't giving up any time on his bike before winter had set in.

Jimmy had experienced a couple different things that summer, and it would be simple to remember the basic lesson: never pour or use gas on an open fire, and the possibility of gas and Styrofoam ever playing together was impossible.

A few years had rolled by, and Jimmy's mother announced another move. It was 1966, and school was about to start. He would be in first grade this year and had a few mixed emotions about new friends, new teachers, and new homework. Although Jimmy still remained just a little excited and couldn't wait to say, "I'm a first grader!"

Little did Jimmy realize his first day of school would be filled with mystery and adventure. The excitement was full of risk, and little did Jimmy know he would be exposed to danger for another time.

They were unable to completely move into their new house before the start date, and they would have to be picked up by Mom from school. The problem was Jimmy's mother had a full-time job and had to pick up his little brother and then pick up the older siblings. With packing, moving, and being a single mother, this was going to be a challenge.

As Jimmy watched the last bus leave the parking lot and the lights being turned off in the school, the feeling of being abandoned became overwhelming as nightfall was approaching fast. They had no idea how long the walk home was, just that it was far away and they should get started before dark.

Everything seemed fine to Jimmy until they were on the free-way. Speeds seemed like they were a hundred miles an hour and dangerous for anyone, especially a six-, eight-, and ten-year-old kid.

After miles of walking, the police arrived, and a nice policeman asked where they were going. Jimmy quickly replied, "Home!"

The policeman smiled and asked, "Where's home?" They all pointed north. With a second smile, the policeman said, "Let's get you home."

Jimmy couldn't wait to ride in the police car, and as far as he was concerned, they could drive around all night.

The car had a really cool radio with other police people talking and really cool flashing lights. Jimmy noticed the respect and care as the other traffic passed by at a slow speed rather than a speed to see who can get home first. When the wheels of the police car rolled in the driveway, Jimmy was relieved that they safely home.

The experience of riding in the police car had replaced the overwhelming feeling of helplessness and uncertainty. Just the fear of being lost was horrifying.

Jimmy had learned something that day.

Choice and opportunity are not always without fear.

The move was finally complete, and Jimmy's new house was nothing short of amazing. It had a big yard, two bedrooms for his mother and sister, and the finished basement for the boys.

Jimmy made new friends quickly, and the new school was filled by a mystery of its own.

The school's detailed brick walls and bright white-framed windows completed the English-style construction as bridges on both sides finished its entry. Its beautiful front yard was filled with big oak trees and the half-moon driveway where the busses would deliver its students.

Jimmy thought it looked like something out of a storybook, and he would soon learn the school came with many years of history. The school still stands today, filled with history of education in its prime.

It was a place where Jimmy learned to be his own person, where he learned excitement for his future, and the importance of being inspired in the education of reading, math, science, and history. School was a place where Jimmy experienced the groundwork that would open doors of opportunity to be anything he wanted to be. A place where hope lined its walls, dreams covered its floors, and happiness was held first and fear was ignored.

The creek below carried fresh water over its rocks, smoothing and polishing its rough surfaces as it passed with life's challenges of rain, snow, and ice.

Each day, it brought new beginnings, rolling, turning, and splashing new energy as its creatures were washed and cleaned.

As each day ended and the sun set below the horizon, its waters became calm as the creek prepared for a new day. Its water carried hope within its surface, dreams within its turns, and the flow of promise for tomorrow.

Jimmy would spend the next six years at the school, and, although not without challenge, he learned about friendship and what it meant to call someone a friend.

How important it is to learn that someone that becomes your friend comes to you fragile and even lacking words at times. To be built like blocks, where you start with strong footings, and as you build, attention to each other provides strength as your friendship grows.

He also learned that education in studies and the disappointments that accompany them were part of his journey, and he would work hard to always have memories beyond his time spent there.

As the school year became summer and the activities of the season entered high gear, Jimmy's dad would pick them up for the weekend at Grandpa and Grandma's house at the lake. Swimming and fishing and a little boating were usually the highlights of their trips.

Everyone couldn't wait to get there. The trip was always an interesting car ride because Jimmy's dad, for the most part, always had a crappy car, without air-conditioning or heat.

Jimmy would wake up early on Saturday as the lake was simply magnificent. The fish never stopped biting, and the excitement of that next big one never got old.

It wasn't long before Jimmy's summer passed like the wind. The fall season arrived, and the leaves began their descent to the ground in brilliant colors of red, orange, yellow, and brown. As the leaves began to cover the surface with different shapes and sizes, Jimmy wondered about the wisdom of a tree.

The leaves that once delivered the wealth of freshness to the air of spring broke loose and gracefully fell to the ground in the fall as they identified their inter beauty with color.

The snow had begun moving across the state, and the excitement began to blend with the touch of wax beneath Jimmy's skis as he would glide quickly down the hill.

Jimmy and his brothers and sister had begun downhill skiing at a very early age, and it was one of the family treasures of the season.

This wasn't talked about much around their dad because it shortened the time they would spend with him, and that was short enough already.

To their surprise, Jimmy's dad had bought snowmobiles that winter, and, of course, that added more excitement than just standing around a hole in the ice, waiting for a fish too bite, not to mention with cold hands and frozen feet.

Jimmy was too young to drive the snowmobiles, although riding around and going fast from time to time was a blast. It mixed the fun and sometimes blended the time between parents, and divorce became the forgotten word. Jimmy continued having difficulty understanding how moms and dads stop loving each other, and sometimes would ask himself, *How is this possible?* He felt guilty, telling his dad how sorry he was about all the time he spent with his mom. He wasn't sure if his dad would stop loving him too.

Although Jimmy had experienced their relationship, which involved kissing, hugging, and love, as a little person at the age of seven, he remained a little confused about how two people can dismantle and disregard something they once called love.

As Jimmy sat quietly on the front steps, looking out at the world in deep thought, he thought about one thing for sure. The way he felt about his parents would never change. They remained the bright light, the safe place where laughter and happiness could be found, even if they weren't together.

Jimmy thought a lot about what happiness and love could be between two people. He imagined it like holding hands, where both become stronger together, although one hand without the other hand seems to cause both to become fragile or weak. The love and hope for each other becomes unknown or distant without a title.

As he consumed the lessons of the good and the bad between people, the minutes filled the hours, shaping each day with continued change. Happiness seems to consume love, or maybe happiness becomes love.

Jimmy discovered although love and happiness can become weakened and crumble like the sand in his sandbox, the love appears to be collected. It's filed away in memories, finding sometimes anger can control both, some for maybe a lifetime and others in the moment.

Is it the footings, is it the walls, or is it the roof?

Jimmy's 525,600 minutes in the year had become the challenge.

As each day ended, the number that sounded so big became the number that remained so small. He spent painless hours on the footings, strengthening the walls as he went. The roof became the victory. The place became the file that appeared to retain the friendship.

"Is the mistreatment of another, the layers between the mounds that cover the wealth of the beginning?"

It was 1967, and the day had begun with a winter storm. The snow was thick and heavy, covering the streets and highways. It rested on tree branches as it began to pile and bend with its weight. The outdoors had become frosty white with very little color, clean and fresh as it piled with mystery.

School was well underway, and Jimmy's days allowed very little playtime, a few snacks, and, of course, homework.

A snow day would change the outcome of the day with lots of playtime as school and homework would quickly be forgotten, maybe even delaying a test or two.

It was that time of year when Jimmy was becoming excited for Christmas as the winter wonders of the snow were welcomed for the ski season and playing in its wonder.

The neighborhood had the best sledding hill in the area. You could choose your own point of entry or level of excitement, and the end destination was on the pond below. This was the place where Jimmy and his friends would meet regularly during the winter months and spend hours having fun and experience some terrifying rides down the hill.

Today the snow was unusual. It seemed to have a plan of its own, and it seemed that kids were not within the plan. Jimmy couldn't put his finger on why he was feeling almost uncomfortable with the snow. Generally, a storm like this would bring extra excitement to the day.

What was the snow trying to say? Where would the wind blow it?

How would it land, and why did Jimmy feel mystery and danger within its path?

CHAPTER 3

Consequence

The next morning, the snow continued to fall, and while Jimmy was getting ready for school, he glanced out the window.

The trees appeared thin as the outline of white surfaces softened its shapes. The ground was covered with a bright white fluffy blanket. Its daylight hours appeared very different than other days. Excitement and uneasiness shared the same space. Jimmy tied his boots, and his thoughts remained and felt strange. When Jimmy stepped through the door into the snow, thoughts seemed to vanish as the school bus took him to the open road.

School had started late because of the storm. To everyone's surprise, the day ended early because buses would struggle to return everyone home. The day became consumed by heavy snowfall. Visibility over the hood of the school bus was about as far as you could see.

The best part of the day was when the teacher mentioned no homework as she hurried all the children to their buses. Jimmy's normal daily chore was to take the trash out to the burn barrel in the backyard and light the match. In those days, the only garbage was cans and glass, and everything else was burned.

Now this was a very big deal for Jimmy. It would be his first year doing the job.

Everyone had just finished dinner and began clearing the table. Jimmy prepared for the trip to the burn barrel located far in the backyard away from the house. When Jimmy opened the door, he stood for a moment in amazement. "Wow" described his excitement, and when his little brother heard him, he had to see too. That's all it took for his little brother to start begging him to take him with.

At first, Jimmy said no, although after "please, please, please," Jimmy said, "All right, get your boots and jacket on and let's go."

When Jimmy's older brother looked out the door, he wanted to go too. So after getting dressed, anticipating some fun in the snow, they all headed out the door.

It was truly like no other snowfall they had ever seen. The flakes were the size of quarters, the air was silent, and the freshness was extraordinary.

Snow piled on tree branches like frosting on cupcakes. The snow was so deep Jimmy's little brother had to follow in his footprints, lifting his leg up to the surface and back down into the hole of the next foot impression. They all began to laugh with joy as they experienced the fun of the snowstorm.

The sky was dark, and it was like the stars were falling from above, mesmerizing as they gently landed on the ground. Beautifully, it was like the sound of soft music as they touched the surface.

Jimmy and his brothers stood still, not saying a word. They raised their heads and waited for flakes to gently land on their faces. They opened their mouths for a taste of the frozen ice falling from the sky.

It was a warm night with very little wind. The snow was perfect for snowballs, and after finally making their way back to the burn barrel, they then began the trip back to the house. It wasn't long before snowballs began to fly, and after throwing a few around, the breeze carried the sounds of their friends down the street. Their laughter became irresistible as they played in the snow.

The temptation was overwhelming to sneak away and throw a few snowballs from across the street to surprise the others, then run home before getting in trouble.

It seemed harmless enough. Jimmy looked down the street again, and the distance seemed far, the darkness of the storm looked angry, and the snow had begun to cover their footsteps.

The feeling of danger reentered Jimmy's mind as he looked at his little brother. They all agreed how fun it would be and began the long journey through the snow, down the street, five houses away.

Jimmy's thoughts continued, and he decided if they stayed on their side of the road, it should be okay. With the courage and fearlessness of young children, the first snowball was thrown across the street, and the fight began. To Jimmy and his brothers, the night was filled with joy and happiness. They laughed as the night became the best night ever.

The heavy snow continued to fall, almost blinding the other side of the road. The fun seemed never-ending, without thought or consideration of anything else in the world.

Jimmy had taken his eyes off his little brother when he bent to pick up more snow. His little brother was struggling to get any snowballs across the street and had decided to bring one to the other side.

Then was when it happened. It became the night that would change their lives forever.

It started with a thump. That was when Jimmy's little brother went flying through the air, landing on the hood of the passing car, and began sliding to the front of the hood as he disappeared out of sight, under the car.

Then another thump as one of Jimmy's little brother's boots was thrown from under the rear of the car.

Time became suspended. Voices and snowfall in slow motion as the car that glided down the roadway had Jimmy's little brother trapped beneath. His tiny body was dragged three hundred feet before the car finally slammed into the snowbank on the shoulder.

Children's laughter in the night became filled with horror. The screams came from beneath the car, filling the silence of the night with helplessness and pain.

The sounds of fear bellowed out, rippling down the street as he was held down by the weight of the car. Jimmy's little brother, hit so hard, dented the car, and it now sat with its broken radiator leaking fluid to his little body.

Jimmy's little brother needed help. The driver of the car reached under to pull him free, although he stopped when the screechy screams of pain filled the air once more with echoing chills of torture.

Jimmy stood in disbelief, unable to feel cold, trembling with the fear of uncertainty. Watchers stood silent. The awful sounds of screams beneath the car vanished into the night.

Jimmy had enormous relief as the first police cars arrived, only to discover they were helpless and unable to remove him from under the car.

Police quickly called for a tow truck to lift the car to access Jimmy's little brother's body. He could see the fear in their faces. They knew his little brother had no time, and medical assistance was needed immediately. Time once more stood still as they waited for the tow truck. The snow began to fall harder.

The flakes were now flickering red from the lights of emergency vehicles.

Then a voice from afar said, "The truck's here." The tears from Jimmy's eyes rolled down his cold face, holding back any sounds in order to hear the cries or any sounds from his little brother underneath the car.

Jimmy looked up, thankful, as the truck moved into position to lift the car.

As the car was carefully lifted, the sounds of emotions began from the many who had waited to help save Jimmy's little brother's life. His five-year-old little body was burned and broken as he laid still in the snow covered in blood, although he appeared alive. Jimmy began to hear the rush of emotions beginning to wave among the medical people with the difficult job of getting him ready to move.

As they made decisions about where to start and began to move quickly, Jimmy realized his brother was holding on to life and had very little time left before he died.

Seeing the fear in their eyes, Jimmy began to cry. He looked for his older brother, although he had already gone home for help. Jimmy could only see their lips move. He was unable to hear their words as he was so overcome with fright, increasingly terrified, and asking himself over and over, *How could this happen? Why did I bring him outside? Jimmy, what have you done? How did you let this happen?"*

Now home, the police soon filled Jimmy's family kitchen, looking for ways to contact his mother, who, as of yet, was unaware of the accident and on her way home in the snowstorm.

In 1967, cell phones weren't an option, and the radio was the communication with the outside world. Someone had come up with the idea to broadcast the accident so that by chance, Jimmy's mother might hear the broadcast and go directly to the hospital.

Doctors had begun the long process of attempting to save the life of Jimmy's little brother. It became necessary to make life-saving decisions quickly and without delay, although approvals for procedures were needed. Jimmy and his brother and sister had been transported to the hospital where they would wait for their mother's arrival and their little brother's outcome. He could see the desperation in the eyes of the doctors. Jimmy began feeling very uncomfortable, and the unthinkable began to set in.

The hospital emergency room was separated by two large swinging doors with long picture-frame-shaped windows that allowed access to the hallway where Jimmy sat and prayed for his mother to walk through those doors. He needed her to walk through those doors.

"Please, Mom, walk through those doors."

Every time the doors would open, it was someone else. Jimmy's faith became distant as his hope became challenged. Jimmy knew the accident was on him. The challenge became the struggle. Jimmy wished it were him fighting for life. He would give anything to take his little brothers place, although Jimmy knew that was impossible. He was willing to give his life for his brother.

The fault of the accident overlaid the cause. To Jimmy, it would become his first mound, complete with guilt, shame, and regret.

Jimmy wanted the time to stand still. The clock on the wall began to turn faster and faster. The visual recall was of his little brother's boot cartwheeling through the air in slow motion after tipping the chrome bumper on the back of the car. The consequences of his choice pressed hard.

Hopelessness and fear were consuming every inch of him.

Then the doors opened as his mother walked through. The skin on her face was pale, her eyes filled with fear, the tears rolled from her cheeks as the doctors whispered her away to where Jimmy's young brother laid, waiting for surgery. The silence became overwhelming, but Jimmy and his brother and sister were comforted by the knowledge that their brother was alive.

The sunrise soon brought daylight. The snow had stopped, and the daytime noises had begun, and it seemed as if Jimmy's little brother would survive.

His right cheek was completely removed. Layers of skin from his chest were removed and cleaned to prevent infection from the burns by the radiator fluid that had dripped to his body.

A cast was placed on his right leg, hip to hip and hip to toe, holding his leg to his body. It had broken in three places when the car slammed into his three-foot body.

Jimmy got to see his little brother only by photo as he was kept in the critical care unit to prevent infection. His burns remained open for further surgery. He was unrecognizable, although he was wrapped in white sheets like angels had come to his rescue. Jimmy was comforted knowing his little brother was not alone. He wanted to stay at his bedside, although he knew it was not possible. The worst part was not knowing when his brother would have the opportunity to have visitors other than his mother.

The recovery time was unknown. Surgery after surgery, placing skin grafts to repair the hole in his cheek would take months in the hospital before Jimmy could visit. He wished he never had to leave him there alone and in pain.

It was 1968 now, and the snow was melting as the winter season was ending.

Jimmy's little brother would be coming home soon, and he would arrive by ambulance. All the furniture from the living room had been removed because it became his new hospital room, with hospital bed and all.

Jimmy had still not talked to his brother about the accident. He feared his little brother would not forgive him, not love him, and not trust him ever again. Jimmy felt the conversation might make him angry. He was scared. His fear inside was real, and the thought made him shake and sick to his stomach.

He had very little doubt that the accident was still fresh within his little brother's mind.

Jimmy had made his final decision. He would say nothing. His prayers for him to come home had been answered, and he would help with whatever his young brother needed, including emptying his bedpan. The cast covered his body hip to hip and down his right leg, restricting his movement, and rolling him to his side placing heat lamps to dry his bed soars was necessary.

Jimmy soon found himself asking if the happiness would return to his home. It seemed absent, lacking measurement and quality.

Jimmy wondered what the new family normal would be like. His thoughts stood still without movement, frozen in time. But he wanted to talk about it; he needed to talk about it. Jimmy wondered if his feelings should be kept inside, forgotten, and never be spoken of again.

Is it possible to forget bad memories, or are they merely banked for another day? Or is it possible memories simply lie between the mounds like a blanket that can be removed?

Jimmy soon wondered if repairing and healing can be found in words, as he unknowingly allowed fear to create walls. Although riddled with hidden pain and struggle, he looked at his little brother with eyes of compassion. He laid there helpless, wounded, and broken, and he knew he had caused this to happen.

Even at eight years old, Jimmy knew right from wrong. He had chosen wrong, and the shame and guilt he felt decided his personal happiness would have to wait.

The big question for Jimmy was, How could he bring happiness to his brother? Showing he cares and loves him, would that be enough?

Jimmy had answered the question without even knowing, although at eight, the will to fight the correct answer appeared normal. Jimmy focused on his pain, his loneliness, and sadness as challenges hopefully would become less each day. Each day would be a new day, and maybe he and his brother would find happiness together like before.

Maybe the unspoken words would become words in measurements; this tragedy along with its pain and struggle would be behind them, although not forgotten as one of life's lessons.

The scar that covers his little brother's cheek would be the reminder that Jimmy would learn to live with, finding some peace that he is alive when all odds were against him.

As he laid blooded and broken on the roadway, the car that had almost taken his life would be the vision that would always be with him.

The accident would remain one of life's greatest unwanted lessons.

As months passed, Jimmy's brother would become stronger, his sadness would become less, and, as painful as it was, he would even smile from time to time.

Although some time had gone by, Jimmy felt separation from his mother. He often felt without hope, endless without understanding, love without forgiveness.

Jimmy would lie quietly in his bed at night, lonely and wishing his mother would just say it.

"You took him outside when you knew it was wrong, and now look at what you've done. This was your fault."

Jimmy felt maybe, just maybe, she would feel better, and maybe then understanding and forgiveness between them or at least conversation could begin. Jimmy's feeling of being unwanted, unneeded, and without purpose continued as the tears from Jimmy's eyes recognized the pain within his very soul.

Jimmy remained close to his brother, doing anything that would make him happy, although with hidden intention.

Jimmy prayed for his brother's forgiveness and love.

He wanted more than anything in the world for his brother to trust him again.

The full cast was finally removed, although doctors wanted the leg to regain some badly needed muscle so they recast just the leg for about two more weeks. This was good news for the whole family, and a trip together to California was in the making and just what everyone needed.

Jimmy's mom had even bought a new station wagon for the trip. It had long windows on both sides of the roof where the views were incredible, and the space inside was amazing.

The doctors agreed they would review x-rays from California where their destination of the trip was scheduled. There they would determine if the cast could be removed. Everything went as planned, and the cast was removed.

Jimmy was very excited. This was the best part of the trip. This would be when his brother would take his first steps.

His steps were gentle due to weakness, but it was like a victory for the whole family.

His little brother's face had his smile back. It was somewhat constricted by his continued healing of injured tissue and skin grafts from the burn to his face, but it was there.

Jimmy's memories of that night were quickly interrupted by his brother's expression of joy and happiness.

He was happy to see his brother walk again, and he knew in time he could run again. It was another miracle.

Would it be okay to cheer for him? Jimmy would ask himself.

He often wondered if it was okay to express happiness and laughter or if it was to be locked in a glass jar only to be opened after forgiveness. Jimmy decided happiness was love, and with overwhelming joy, he cheered on his brother with support as he walked across the room.

The trip became the first step of healing for the entire family. Everyone knew it was going to take some time before the memories of that night and the year that had impacted the very essence of happiness or the abundance of happiness that once filled their home.

Jimmy knew that his little brother would be reminded of that night for the rest of his life whenever he felt or saw the scar on his face.

The vision of what happened on that snowy night would never be erased from his memory.

Jimmy prayed that the hopes and dreams his little brother was born with would never be forgotten and he would be inspired by life itself.

The accident was never talked about again, although Jimmy's curiosity always wondered if his little brother realized how close to death he had been.

Would he ever want to learn about that night, or would learning about the unspoken be harmful?

Jimmy found himself fearful, stuck between helpful and harmful. The very idea of speaking the words and hearing the contents of the story brought emotions to the surface. Jimmy had relived the seconds and minutes and hours of what appeared to be a lifetime of memories without ending.

The regret of the choice would remain forever, but the unwillingness to forgive oneself completed another mound of hidden disappointment.

Can forgiving yourself possibly be the key to freedom?

CHAPTER 4

Unexpectedly

It was the summer of 1968, and Jimmy's family had returned from the long-needed vacation. It appeared to reenergize some happiness and joy back into everyone.

The trip was long, and everyone was glad when the car pulled into their driveway. The time away from friends and just missing their own beds brought some shared excitement.

It had been some time since the family had reached outside their family environment. The pain and challenge of the accident had consumed their daily routine, and Jimmy recognized the need for everyone to reconnect with the outside world.

Jimmy had decided to go down to the neighbor's house and meet up with friends. It was a beautiful day, and the sun was magnifying the bright fall colors.

As Jimmy walked toward the neighbor's house, he saw the kids were playing tag, and Jimmy quickly joined in the fun.

The game soon became the older boys against the younger boys, and they came up with an idea that would change Jimmy's life once again.

They came up with the idea to pull the garage door down and stand on the two-inch metal ledge at the bottom of the door, holding it from opening.

As the older boys came around the house and discovered their plan, they began pulling up on the door. Their plan seemed to be working until Jimmy's friend's felt the door leave the ground, and they jumped off the ledge. Up went the door with Jimmy still on it.

It happened so fast Jimmy was unable to jump off and fell to the concrete headfirst. He stood, feeling like the lights had gone out. A little dizzy, he placed his hand on the back of his head. The bump was already growing, and it felt like the size of a large egg. As Jimmy stood for a second, he realized he was injured and closed his eyes in pain. With tears in his eyes, Jimmy knew the game was over and he needed to go home.

The boys asked Jimmy if he was okay.

"I'm okay, I'm going home."

When Jimmy arrived home, he immediately laid down in his bed, feeling like his head was going to explode. He knew something was terribly wrong. Although frightened, he remained in bed.

Jimmy laid as still as he could, wishing for some relief, asking it to please go away, like most young kids do. What seemed to be only a short time turned into three hours later. When Jimmy didn't show for dinner, his mother came looking and found him lying on his bed in his dark bedroom. She placed her hand on his shoulder, and he opened his eyes. He wasn't sure how long he was there, and his first thought was he must have fallen asleep.

Jimmy turned his head and was quickly reminded of the fall and the bump on the back of his head. His eyes began to push forward from his face. His lips appeared to be awkward as he looked at his mother.

She asked if he was okay and if he was coming to dinner. Jimmy said he wasn't very hungry and began telling his mother about what had happened and showed her the bump on his head. She quickly went to the freezer for ice.

After some time had passed, Jimmy's mother had decided to take him to the hospital. This was the same hospital where Jimmy's little brother was saved, and it gave some comfort as the fear of survival began to take root, and he felt he would be in good hands.

The doctors completed their tests and came back with the discovery of a brain bleed on the back of Jimmy's head. Due to the time that had passed, the bleeding had clotted and stopped. The doctor placed his hand on Jimmy's shoulder and told him he would be fine, although the need for observation would be necessary just in case the bleeding reoccurred.

What had started out to be another day of fun accompanied by joy, happiness, and laughter brought injury and another day that would soon change Jimmy's life.

The doctor gave Jimmy's mother some medication and told her the clot should slowly dissolve and surgery would not be necessary.

The next day, Jimmy told his mother he felt better, and the pressure was not as bad as the day before. Then, unexpectedly, Jimmy zoned out.

His mother began tapping him, finally shaking him by the shoulders to get his attention.

His mother looked at him and asked him why he wasn't answering her. She then realized something was very wrong and returned Jimmy to the hospital.

The doctor began testing again. After the tests were completed, the doctor came in and explained the new diagnosis. Jimmy was having petit mal seizures caused by the brain injury, and they prescribed medication that would assist with his recovery and would probably be required for an unknown amount of time.

Jimmy had very little idea what the doctor was saying, and he started to ask questions. The doctor tried to help Jimmy understand the situation, but listening was like he was daydreaming, although not the good kind where pleasant and wishful imagination occurs.

It was like he was suspended in time, unknowingly tuned out to the world, unable to hear or acknowledge the things happening and words around him.

Jimmy became overwhelmed with fear, wishing he had never stepped on to the ledge of the door or at least jumped from the door like the other guys.

The damage to Jimmy's brain became the consuming thoughts of the uncertainty of tomorrow. He was only eight years old at the time, and now the injury was never going away. His new world was filled with unknowns.

The circumstance that happened in a flash of light that was uncontrollable, unstoppable, and unprotected carried the end result with no return. Or so he felt.

Fear quickly filled Jimmy's mind.

Would he be normal? Or would he be stupid? Or would people know? Or would people look at him differently?

Jimmy realized something very quickly. With all these thoughts in his mind, his head was still connected to his body.

His eyes could still see the world. He looked okay in the mirror. That's got to be a good thing.

Although Jimmy felt cursed, and maybe even deserving, he was applying this as unfinished business about his little brother's accident.

Jimmy's brain injury, requiring medication three times a day, and with unknown consequences, would be Jimmy's first experience with unwanted fear—the kind God didn't intend.

It's the type of fear that brings loneliness, rejection, and judgment, encompassing shame, humiliation, and disappointment. The fear that can be manipulated by people. Thoughtlessness and lack of compassion, with the possibility that it could be used as a hurtful tool against him was frightening. Sadness began nesting within Jimmy.

The school year was beginning, and the extra anxiety of preparing for his first day was very uncomfortable. When most are filled by excitement of new clothes and school supplies, Jimmy was filled with worry. The last thing he cared about was how he looked or the pattern on his notebook covers. He would be required to inform his teacher about his condition in order for him to get his medication from her at lunchtime. Jimmy made every effort to let his teacher know he was uncomfortable about it, yet she would still call him to the front of the room.

"Jimmy, it's time for your medication."

He would always tip his head to the ceiling and thank God for the bell because sometimes they wouldn't be able to hear or pay attention to her calling him to the front of the room.

The year was 1969, and Jimmy was in the fourth grade. Times were different then. It was when teachers could still hit you with the pointer stick, or the three-foot ruler better known as a yardstick.

Sometimes if you were lucky, you would simply just stand in the corner, facing the wall.

Jimmy fearlessly, not being able to avoid humiliation, went to the front of the room to retrieve his medication. If he didn't know better, he thought the teacher looked disappointed when Jimmy would smile and say thank you as he went to lunch.

Things would get better for Jimmy over time. Medication became a normal daily activity almost without much thought.

As this school year ended, Jimmy and his brothers and sister were excited about seeing their father and going to the lake.

They would regularly stop for ice cream and haircuts on the way, and even though the haircuts were to the skin, Jimmy always looked forward to spending time with his dad in the boat, catching fish.

The only problem was Jimmy didn't care much for using the can in the boat to pee in because the boat avoided the return to the dock until just before dark.

The weekend was like most. Fishing, lots of food, swimming in the lake, playing in the yard, and, of course, Grandma's cookies. Little did everyone know this weekend would be far different than most.

It all started with lunchtime when Jimmy's little brother went into the house to tell everyone, "Jimmy's sleeping in the sandbox."

To his fathers' surprise, as he walked up on the sandbox, sure enough, Jimmy was sleeping inside it. As you can imagine, anybody sleeping in the sandbox in the middle of the day can be a bit strange and scary all at the same time.

Jimmy's brothers and sister stood in amazement. What was happening with their brother? Lunch quickly became the forgotten part of the day, and the urgency to get Jimmy to the hospital unfortunately replaced the afternoon at the lake.

It had been another great day covered by blue sky and only a few clouds lingering high above, and the sun warmed the air. The day was filled with fun and joyful laughter, although again, it changed in a single moment.

Jimmy was quickly loaded into the car. They started for the hospital as he began to wake in the lap of his father asking him what happened. Jimmy had no memory of anything and only said, "I'm cursed, and I think we need to call my mom."

After arriving at the hospital, Jimmy was tested for his brain injury, and it was determined he had a grand mal seizure.

It had not been part of any family conversation. His medications always reminded him he was different than the other kids, and without it, he knew many different problems could occur.

While retaining his secret became easier, the problem that stirred within Jimmy's emotions became difficult to understand. The space where it appears, brain injuries automatically become the category of brain damage or stupidity, or maybe even crazy, to most of the population, Jimmy believed. He held the possibility of judgment in the palm of his hand. He recognized the way a person feels about oneself can have many repercussions.

The slow recovery in the sandbox was normal, although Jimmy would need further care from his neurologist.

It was also possible that without Jimmy's medication, it had triggered the episode since he had forgotten it at home. Jimmy's dad was unaware of the situation because Jimmy was caring for himself, and his medication was routine and as normal as brushing his teeth in the morning and at night.

The doctors at the lake hospital had discussed his problems with Jimmy's mother on the phone and issued medication to cover the amount needed for the weekend.

Jimmy apologized to his dad and everyone else with a hidden level of embarrassment and humiliation.

He was disappointed. The frustration and his vision of tomorrow suddenly became uncertain. His hopes and dreams became more distant and almost unachievable as he slept for the rest of the day.

He asked himself when he woke, *How can this be possible? How can the experience of happiness and the excitement of life, where everything is good and the way life should be, turn into a day of loneliness, lacking life's ingredient of joy?*

Jimmy had discovered over time he should make every attempt to be happy. The new day, in most cases, was filled with mystery and the promise of discovery, and as hard as anyone tries to repeat a day, it just isn't possible.

Jimmy remained without every answer. Like always, he hated the feeling of being different than everyone else, although he continued moving forward. His hopes were that it wouldn't happen again.

He was struggling to accept the fact medication would most likely be the norm for him. That had created another challenge. Jimmy, although saddened and wishing the fall never happened, was thinking about how he had changed his little brother's life. Why should his be any different?

Jimmy would soon unknowingly struggle throughout another major event that would be far different than his image or his health. His mother announced she was getting remarried.

The announcement to the family came with a little lack of enthusiasm and was noticed as Jimmy looked around the room and the faces of questions appeared.

The house, the street, and the changes that everyone had worked through began piling up, and as small children, they had accepted many things, although having the willingness to replace their dad was not one of them.

Even though Jimmy and his brothers and sister showed lack of approval, any different outcome seemed unlikely. And it appeared their mother was very happy, as her face glowed and her smile reached for acceptance.

The happiness of their mom was always important to them. Their mother also struggled throughout the many changes herself.

The loneliness she experienced as a single mom appeared to be absent, and the glow of happiness appeared to be present.

After some time, she announced they would be moving again, and that became a little more challenging for everyone.

Life began to take the shape of constant change, and the changes so far had the shape of a large abstract painting, where everything mashes together, and although it can be very beautiful, it has very little rhyme or reason.

To Jimmy, the marriage was bad enough. Now they were going to move again, have to make new friends, and attend a new school. Those thoughts made the announcement even harder to accept.

Jimmy began notifying his friends of their plans to move to a new house. The disappointment was shared by families and friends in the neighborhood.

Everyone had experienced some shape or form of Jimmy's little brother's accident. The families throughout the neighborhood shared something far greater than most families should ever have to share. When children begin holding on to life, it changes who we are as people, exposing vulnerability, making values become different, and making simple life become challenging. But the community becomes stronger, and the love and care for each other gets ingrained. Jimmy began growing up way too fast and dealing with life-changing events at a very early age, distracting the normal growing process.

Jimmy had learned that within one second, life can be altered beyond any control, and in the process, some gifts can be filled by gratitude and others covered with doubts and sadness.

Moving from the neighborhood, Jimmy had realized the love and the care from the friends and families there. He was gifted something he was never aware of or appreciated.

A deposit in the bank of wealth. Dreams filled with love.

CHAPTER 5

Magnificent

As Jimmy's mother attempted to make the transition acceptable for the family, she looked at homes in the same area and within the same school district.

Soon Jimmy and his brothers and sister learned they would only be moving across the highway, remaining in the same district, and the new house had an indoor swimming pool that made the choice a little more exciting. Jimmy began thinking the move might be a good thing. Moving away from the tragedies in the neighborhood could just be the motivator to move forward for everyone.

After some time, the memories of the old house became just that—a memory. The family settled in and began making new friends. Jimmy, although loyal to his dad, with undecided feelings, looked for some kind of happiness through it all. He was ten years old at the time. He still struggled with the unknown journey of each day no matter how exciting each measurement throughout the day became. It's just the way life delivers its lessons.

Jimmy's days with undiscovered happiness and with never-ending dreams of the future became the focus. Not always easy and often involved struggle, the endurance and acceptance of change was making him stronger.

Can dreams be as simple as endurance and acceptance of change?

With the many experiences of Jimmy's young childhood, acceptance continued to be the conflict. He held it within his wealth of youthful knowledge. Although over time, it appeared to find hidden spaces where memories and lessons temporarily become forgotten wealth. Places where the wealth he had earned became banked in his emotional bank account.

Jimmy's acceptance of change had become the lock on his account. Although he unknowingly held the imaginary key in his pocket, it wasn't tangible yet.

As time moved on, Jimmy learned he didn't like the water much, even with the indoor pool. Although after being thrown off the dock and learning how to swim for survival, he did learn how to water-ski.

Within a short time, Jimmy's family began participating in professional ski competition. He found himself frustrated at times because he felt he wasn't very good. After many attempts, he became comfortable on his water skis, just as he was on snow skis. Serious and exciting changes in performance were happening.

What a discovery.

This was very exciting to Jimmy, and although practice made the summer a little shorter, it was filled with enjoyment, and Jimmy's efforts started to pay off.

He had learned good things come with the cost of hard work and disappointments. Maybe this time, happiness could last forever.

What a thought.

The end of the summer came quickly, and school would be starting soon. The water ski season was ending, and winter wasn't far off. The lakes soon became ice-covered, and the ground was covered in snow.

Frigid temps weren't Jimmy's favorite, although snow skiing was starting soon, and the family was all into skiing, and every Saturday, they would travel to different ski parks.

It was truly amazing to Jimmy when they visited new ski areas because they would meet so many new people.

Jimmy was never shy and would continually engage in conversations with anyone. He had learned and found most will always exchange words, although many wonder why you would ever want to talk to them or just simply feel awkward.

The awkward feeling was okay because Jimmy had the ability to work with the uncomfortable feeling most have when meeting new people.

Jimmy would quickly find a topic of interest and would also recognize when people just weren't very interested in conversation.

The funniest place Jimmy liked to talk with people is in the elevator. He would say something like, "Is it just me, or do we all look at the numbers, hoping for some famous voice to go with them?"

Jimmy always found this is a great place to inspire conversation with people and move outside of their comfort zone. Inspiring smiles and laughter make it a better day or even a great day. Jimmy found most are very grateful when you say the first word.

How awkward could it be, trapped in an elevator, six feet by six feet, and have someone bring up conversation only to discover your own vulnerability as you experience the joy and happiness that others bring to life in that sixty-second ride?

What an exciting discovery. Check it out sometime. Recognize the feeling you get when you arrive at your destination. Even if they are grumpy and change is not noticeable, their thought of the day has changed. You made their day better.

Interruption of thought, what a concept.

Jimmy loved to stay busy throughout the winter and would play basketball and attend Boy Scout meetings one day a week, with an occasional campout sometime in the summer.

With the signs of winter beginning to vanish and spring approaching fast, Jimmy realized school and basketball had dominating most of his time.

Jimmy had recognized the friendships he made and the friendships he already had, and the fun and laughter shared became so different when people are separated for the summer.

Although the summer was only for a short time and most stayed connected with a few friends, Jimmy began to learn the importance and strength of love in friendships was the strength in joy and happiness.

Notice the smile within yourself the next time you think of your friend, the experience, the joy, the happiness, and the love. Pay attention to the hidden or forgotten wealth within yourself, the kindness, the laughter, and the excitement.

As Jimmy prepared for the upcoming water ski season, it would require him in the water by mid-April.

It's a time when the water is less than favorable for the human body. The first tournament was in the third week in May, and he was determined to be ready.

His water skis became like a collection of precious treasures, filled with memories of every win and every loss. Jimmy learned that happiness, hope, dreams, and excitement can also be filled with sadness and disappointments of one's performances. Although necessary for people to grow and thoughts move you forward like God intended, nowhere is it written you can't be pissed off!

Jimmy had turned eleven years old this year, and he would be in the division where the competition would be a little more challenging than usual. This would require Jimmy to practice every day to get ready for the season. In many instances, Jimmy seemed more joyful, happier, and filled with laughter when he was introduced to new challenges.

Things that continued to remind him of his many blessings in life were important because although Jimmy had a brain injury, he wanted people to recognize that quality as a person.

Even at eleven, the thought of being treated differently because of his injury was threatening to his performance. Jimmy only wanted the best he could achieve, the person he wanted to be, although he was distracted by the need for overachievement.

Jimmy had spent his fair share of time thinking he had to prove himself to everyone, hoping and believing most would see the qualities within him. In a short time, he had learned that people that were aware of his injury treated him differently. Concealment was easier than just saying "I have a brain injury that causes seizures. I take medications. It doesn't make me crazy, and it doesn't make me stupid."

He knew in the world he lived in, if people didn't think it through, they would just feel sorry for you.

Judgment can become primary, or easier, and feeling lucky they are not like you becomes secondary. Jimmy always wanted people to notice and recognize the way they viewed people or talked about people with disability, obesity, or other challenges. Acceptance, dignity, understanding, or compassion and integrity works both ways. He believed most people feel a little guilty by their thoughts. Being thankful they are not like you comes with humility or embarrassment.

In most cases, Jimmy experienced people going through times like he did, when feeling sorry for yourself consumes your thoughts, and the hopelessness about any given condition. It seems to interfere with the pursuit of love for the way you feel about yourself.

The doctors generally want to diagnose depression or sadness and treat with medications. Jimmy believed getting out of your head was the only challenge, and medications should be the last resort for comfort.

Jimmy wouldn't wish his condition on his worst enemy and was thankful the many people he knew were not in his situation. He began to understand the challenges. He had learned about bulling at early ages in his life. The discovery of the mistreatment of others and the lack of consequences became the lessons learned.

Jimmy has tripped over many people that are mistreated or unfairly judged.

People with the same hopes and dreams we are all born with, filled with more love and kindness than many without challenge.

As Jimmy sat on the end of the dock, waving his legs, tiptoeing skips across the surface of the water, he imagined the large amount of wealth we are born with that becomes covered by mounds of unresolved and sometimes complicated journeys.

The discoveries of the walls many stand behind that are created by circumstance, and although God's gift for survival is meant to protect them, their struggle becomes the fragile walls that are filled with holes. Weak over time, without repair, the possibility of holding the weight of the roof to victory becomes like predicting the future.

Jimmy believes most should be proud of living in a world where people with challenges fight to be the most they can be, even though they know their condition draws attention.

A place where everyone continues learning. They can be reminded continually of God's many gifts that can become completely unnoticed or forgotten as life can strip them away from us in a single moment.

CHAPTER 6

Punishment

It was early evening, and everyone had just finished dinner. Jimmy, along with his brothers and sister, had a little free time to watch television or do whatever came to mind, and this wasn't very often. Then, without warning, loud voices filled the house like an echo in a hollow cannon. Horrifying screams of an argument consumed any other sounds in the house. The sounds came from Jimmy's mothers' bedroom.

Quickly, the memories of argument flashed before Jimmy. He hurried to see what was happening, although when he reached his mothers' bedroom, it was empty. Blood droplets laid on its hardwood floor, leading to the table next to her bed where Jimmy found a big shiny silver flashlight on the table, with blood on its end. Jimmy stood still, and his imagination began to wonder. He ran to the garage only to find the family car had already gone.

Jimmy and his brothers and sister waited quietly, without words, sitting for hours at the top of the stairs. They remained uncertain of what had happened. Fear of the unknown once again consumed Jimmy's thoughts.

Where have they gone? When will they be back? Jimmy's eyes filled with tears, and the fear he had not felt in a long time returned.

"Please, Mom, walk through that door."

When the sound of the garage door began to open, the suspense became unbearable. Jimmy's mother entered with a bandage on her forehead, looking worried as she told them all to go to bed. Jimmy quickly asked what happened.

She replied that she fell and hit her head on the table and then told them to please go to bed. As they all went off to bed, knowing she had not told the truth, the worry they all felt remained untouched, unspoken, and unresolved.

Is she afraid? Who is this man she has married?

Jimmy wondered who would hurt the person they love and how people fight to the point where injury and pain become the solution to the problem.

The next day, to Jimmy's surprise, the house seemed quiet—too quiet. His mother said everything was fine when they asked if she was okay.

Jimmy couldn't hold it in any longer. What about the blood on the floor and the big shiny flashlight?

"Whose big flashlight is that?"

His mother continued to show stress in her face and fear in her eyes, although she repeated what she had said the night before.

"I fell and hit my head. I don't know anything about the flashlight."

That's when Jimmy knew. He had hit her with the flashlight, and fear was blocking the truth. Jimmy never asked about the flashlight again, although he did go back to her room, and the flashlight was nowhere to be found. He didn't know what he would do with it when he found it, but he did know he would do anything for his mother to never get hit with it again.

Jimmy noticed things had changed after that, and his mother surprisingly began conversations about the man becoming their stepfather and changing their names.

Her happiness and excitement seemed genuine, as if the argument never happened. Further confusion remained as Jimmy tried to understand how love could continue after acts of violent treatment against the person you share love with. How can love and happiness blend with mistreatment?

Is hurtful behavior blinded by love, and the false appearance of happiness and forgiveness a cover for fear?

And then again, a couple of nights later, while Jimmy sat quietly in his room, the house suddenly filled with argument, and the disagreement began to get louder. Jimmy softly and slowly crept down the hallway to escape being noticed. Around the corner, his older brother was fighting with him.

Jimmy noticed the man's own fingers doubled into the palm of his hand, his thumb crossing over his pointer finger as the color of his fist became pale and the tint of red became noticeable. Jimmy stood quietly as that fist was thrust toward his brother's face.

His brother was standing on the lower step just below the landing, raising his arm to block the hit, and the sound of cracking knuckles surrounded the room.

Silence. Without a word, the man went to the garage, and the sound of the car leaving the driveway seemed to release Jimmy's feet. He wanted to jump up and down in celebration of his brother's victory, although he went to his room without saying a word. Jimmy was confused about what just happened and hoped he was gone and would never be coming back.

Later that day, the garage door opened. Jimmy ran to tell his mother everything that had happened only to find that it was he who had returned.

Jimmy quickly turned away, avoiding eye contact, thinking he would be next. He quietly returned to his room. He smiled to himself walking down the hallway because that man's hand was wrapped in a bandage.

The fight had stopped quickly.

Is it over? Did the injury solve the problem or was it to be continued?

Jimmy sat quietly in his room just across the hallway from his brother's room. Suspense and the silence became annoying as fear became the norm.

Can it be so simple for fear to block and scramble reality?

Jimmy began thinking about fighting and when a person hits another, or when yelling at someone or screaming at someone with hurtful words holds the intention of injecting fear.

Is it because people have learned fear is dominating and powerful?

The next day, Jimmy hoped they would have a discussion about the fight. Maybe he would understand what the argument was about. Not a word was ever said.

Fear had taken control, and Jimmy had found himself in an argument with no idea of its contents. Jimmy thought for a moment.

Do they think I'm too young to talk about what I had seen, or was it even important?

Jimmy figured they were protecting him, and that was pretty cool, so he didn't say anything. Then the next day became interesting when Jimmy's mother wanted him to dress in his church clothes and fix his hair.

He asked his mother where they were going because it wasn't Sunday, and he wasn't aware of any special occasions.

As his brothers loaded in the car, his mom explained, "We have to go see a man about changing your last name." Jimmy quickly replied he didn't want to be adopted or change his last name.

Clear understanding of the turmoil within Jimmy's house began to take shape. He buttoned his shirt and put on his shoes as everyone waited patiently. Okay, maybe not patiently, just using normal conversation to hurry Jimmy along and get him into the car.

"Is my dad going to be there? Does he know about this?" Jimmy asked.

Jimmy's mom replied they were not being adopted. It was only for their name change. "And, yes, your dad does know, and I do not know if he will be there."

As he entered the car and closed his door, the car started down the driveway, and the silence of the car ride became a little awkward. The driveway was very long and surrounded by beautiful tall trees, and as the car made the bends and curves approaching the roadway, Jimmy's mind became consumed, wishing he had talked with his dad before this day.

Jimmy watched out the car window as he passed the houses of his neighborhood, thinking of the many changes with many new beginnings. He noticed the colors of the houses turning from white to blue to brown to gray and then white again. Like a storybook, where the story's pages are filled with adventure, excitement, and inspiration. The question was whether or not the last page was filled with happiness and joy.

Jimmy wanted the day to be filled with the same story, although how would the last page be filled?

He knew one thing for sure—a name change would most likely change the identity of who he would become as a person, where the pages of the book would redefine his story.

Jimmy felt after changing the story halfway through so many times, he recognized the last pages of his story were unwritten with purpose, without thought, unfinished, unknown, and unplanned.

It appeared that judgment that is misguided is built in, learned as life throws its blows, without a plan or reason. As many think, our journey is interrupted for a purpose or reasons unknown.

Jimmy believes life is meant for discovery, and the mystery of our journey is intentional and possibly God's plan.

Jimmy also believes God's gifts have already been given, and all that is needed is a shoulder to cry on. There is support to the process of healing, like now when life tumbles out of control.

Jimmy was still very young, and life quickly became like a ride at the state fair, although lacking the stop button when you wanted the ride to be over.

They soon arrived at this big building with smooth gray walls, windows lined with brick, and doors made of shiny metal, the color of new pennies.

The hallways seemed hollow, its floors covered with colored sprinkles and elevators like cages made of black steel with penny-colored buttons.

Its walls appeared without hope, the floors without dreams, and a place where life changes without choice. Jimmy walked its hallways, rode in its elevator, and entered this really big room with a big desk, where a really nice man asked them to be seated.

Jimmy looked around the room with some unfavorable results. He did not see his dad. He began feeling uncomfortable as he realized his dad was not going to show up at all.

The room suddenly became larger. The windows were like giants, standing tall, trimmed with oak and long curtains from floor to ceiling. Tall trees and vacant spaces filled the view.

Where are you, Dad?

As he continued to look around the room, the next thing he knew, the man behind the desk, with his deep, low, strong voice, asked Jimmy to stand up. Jimmy stood slowly to his feet, his legs feeling shaky, almost weak. He was hoping that at the last minute, his dad would walk in the room.

The question came echoing in Jimmy's mind, although he was not hearing the words.

"Jimmy, do you want to change your last name?"

Jimmy stood silent, terrified as he took one last look around the room. He looked at his mom, stalling for time, and the nice man repeated the question, "Jimmy, do you want to change your last name?"

Jimmy looked at his mom again as he answered with a weak affirmative, although the man asked Jimmy to look at him and answer the question.

Jimmy looked his direction and answered, "Yes, sir."

The nice man thanked Jimmy and asked him to take a seat.

Jimmy began to feel dishonest about his answer. He began to shuffle in his chair, thinking to himself, *Dad, don't you love me?*

Jimmy didn't want anyone to be hurt, especially his mom. Things had been better, and he thought it was just a name and he could always change it back.

The paperwork was completed, although his stepfather didn't look very happy with Jimmy's attitude about the whole thing.

Later, Jimmy had an opportunity to contact his dad. Although Jimmy remained disappointed about his absence, his dad told him he was unaware of the procedure.

Sadly, Jimmy told him that his name was changed with a little bit of anger.

This conversation created a new problem for Jimmy because unknowingly, his new stepfather had overheard Jimmy's conversation with his father, and Jimmy would soon discover the undeserved punishment of his disrespect.

Jimmy's phone call to his dad was for two reasons.

The first was the guilt he felt of changing his name and wanting his dad to know it wasn't because he didn't love him. Unfortunately, Jimmy had expressed it with anger as many children would do.

The second was just anger. If he had loved his mother and they were still together, maybe his life would be different. His mother and father had changed his life with pages of fear, disappointment, and unhappiness.

Jimmy went to bed that night and would soon find out the cost of his disrespect. He shared the room with his little brother, and the lights had just been turned off. The next thing Jimmy knew, he was being held down by the neck, his pillow covering his face, and he was punched over and over again as his body began to wiggle.

The pillow was set aside. Jimmy, with little understanding, gasped for air as he heard the door close and felt its wind blow across the room, leaving its silence darker than before.

The next sound Jimmy heard was the whisper of his little brother, "Are you okay?"

As Jimmy trembled in disbelief of what just happened, he asked himself if his mother thought his punishment was acceptable. With the pain rippling through his face and difficulty opening his jaw, he answered his brother, telling him, "I'm okay."

Jimmy rolled over, trembling throughout his whole body. The blows to the head appeared to rattle his thoughts like scrambled eggs in a bowl with dull edges. His face was tender as it touched his pillow. He cried himself to sleep.

The next morning, when Jimmy and his little brother woke up, they looked at each other, wishing they were remembering a bad dream.

Although Jimmy laid wounded, his face remained tender as the memories and fear remained real. He asked his little brother not to say anything to protect him, and he stayed there for a while.

He looked at the ceiling, hoping and praying with tears in his eyes that it was over, that he was not going to come back for more.

Confused and worried, Jimmy began thinking about what he had done to deserve this punishment.

What kind of person can hold a kid down by the neck and place a pillow over his face while punching him repeatedly?

Who can do this and feel good about it when they're done?

Jimmy wondered about the name-change thing, although he didn't see a lot of reason other than he overheard him talking with his dad.

Was his disappointment enough to treat him like a punching bag, or was it simply fearing the lack of dominating power?

CHAPTER 7

Anticipating

As days and weeks passed, things seemed normal, although Jimmy remained uneasy. His mother seemed happy, and everyone was preparing for the next water ski competition.

Jimmy was working hard on his slalom ski readiness, completing the zigzag course three to four times a day.

Jimmy and his brothers and sister would generally ski three to four hours every day, and this would not leave a lot of time for hanging out with friends.

He had another seizure-free year, and he was always happy about that, although the medications continued to fatigue him from time to time and acted as a reminder that he was sick. Jimmy would oftentimes mention the fatigue to his doctors. Sadly, with Jimmy's condition, medications were required, and the side effects were far better than uncontrollable seizures.

Jimmy's mom and her husband were at work a lot, and this made homelife a little more comfortable for the whole family. His brothers and his sister would practice for their ski season most days after school and throughout the summer.

This would allow very little time with friends just doing kids' stuff. Although opportunities like bad weather or some other commitment would provide time for Jimmy to hang out with friends.

Jimmy had met a girl along the way. She was smart and had long dark hair and a wonderful smile, and the best part of all, she liked competitive sports, like basketball, baseball, and, yes, who could spit the farthest. Jimmy hadn't kissed a girl yet, although if he did, he wanted his first kiss to be from her.

The school year would be starting soon, and this would give Jimmy more time to spend with her and the many friends he had not seen during the summer months. The basketball season was starting soon, and the water ski season was about to end. Jimmy did very well this year. Placing second in many events was a major achievement. He had many trophies to show for the 1972 season.

The school year had started, and with weekends open, Jimmy had time to get together with friends. A friend had asked him to have a sleepover, and after talking with his mom, he packed up the necessary things, and he was off.

They were having a blast and decided to go over to one of their other friend's houses for a little while and shoot some hoops. Just by chance, Jimmy's new girlfriend would be there. After throwing the ball around and shooting some hoops, they had decided to take a break and have some munches and beverages. While conversation and laughter consumed the room, one of the happiest times of Jimmy's life happened just like in his dreams.

Jimmy kissed his first girl. Although it was just a peck, it still counted, and Jimmy couldn't be happier.

After that, they held hands, and this was a pretty big deal for Jimmy. He couldn't help but act a little goofy.

Jimmy believes when two people hold each other's hands, they blended as one, happiness becomes love, and love becomes happiness. It was official. Jimmy had a girlfriend, and his world just became a whole lot better.

Jimmy had known the idea about the responsibility of having a girlfriend. They were both young, and he really didn't know if he was even kissing the correct way, although it appeared to Jimmy she wasn't complaining.

They all sat around talking for a while, and, without warning, the sound of Jimmy's bike landing in the back of the pickup truck parked in the driveway was heard by everyone.

One of Jimmy's friends was frightened and let Jimmy know his dad was there. He stood up quickly, and, with a slight turn, the flat hand to his face square in the nose and mouth knocked Jimmy down to the floor in front of all his friends.

Jimmy laid on the ground, stunned by the blow. He did hear the sounds of his friends gasping with terror and disbelief of what was happening.

Helpless and afraid of what was next for Jimmy, his friends feared of what was next for them as the man had walked right into someone's home uninvited and began beating up Jimmy. Unable to stand, he climbed to his hands and knees. His shirt was grabbed from the back, behind the neck, and he was lifted from the floor like a rag doll as Jimmy was dragged out of the house, hitting every corner, even the range in the kitchen, on the way out the door.

His friends remained horrified and asked Jimmy if they should call the police as he was thrown into the front seat of the truck. They were gone before he could answer.

Jimmy sat very still without words, remaining stunned and out of focus. He was hoping to just get home and for his mom to be there to save him from whatever this was or at least make him stop.

Jimmy feared the unknown and began looking at the door handle, contemplating jumping from the moving vehicle, careful not to look his direction. Fear had control, and he began to tremble. Suddenly, without warning, a backhand to his face made Jimmy aware he was in trouble. With the numbness and what felt like a fat lip, Jimmy, with a slur in his speech, asked, "What are you doing?"

The next backhand hit Jimmy in the nose, and it started to bleed. Jimmy reached to pinch his nose only to find out it was delicate to touch and painful to handle.

He again looked at the door handle, checking the lock on the door, and thought about just doing it, jumping into the roadway and taking his chance of survival. His stepdad began to drive faster and faster, taking away any opportunity of Jimmy's escape.

As the truck arrived at the driveway, Jimmy was thankful. The garage door opened, and his mom's car was not in the garage. He thought to himself when the truck stopped, *I'm going to run. Anticipating whatever this is, it's not good.*

It was like he knew what Jimmy was thinking. He grabbed his arm firmly. He stopped the truck and pulled Jimmy from the front seat, dragging him out the driver's door. He brought him to where the boiler room was located on the back side of the garage. Jimmy's nose was still bleeding. His hands, face, and shirt were covered in blood. He began to think, *This is it, I'm going to die.*

Jimmy was thrown to the concrete floor like a dirty rag as he was told to stay there. The door slammed shut. Looking up, he could see phone-listening devices connected to the phone lines in the house. Jimmy began realizing something was seriously wrong with this guy. Jimmy's fear of the unknown became overwhelming. Helplessness and the thought of death began to take over his body. His mind was rumbling as he screamed for help but got no answers.

Jimmy could hear the garage door going down as someone entered the house. Jimmy sat on the concrete floor as his body trembled and tears poured from his eyes.

This would be Jimmy's chance to escape. He entered the garage. His tears rinsed blood drops to the floor, and he discovered the garage door had been disconnected.

This can't be happening. He said to himself, *It's like something out of a scary movie* as he went for the service door to the house.

As Jimmy reached for the light switch inside the door, his hand was grabbed, and he was dragged to the floor and down the lower hallway.

Jimmy was only twelve years old, so he obviously was over-powered. Frightened and beaten, held by his neck, as his pants were unsnapped and pulled from his body.

He puts Jimmy's member in his mouth and started abusing him. Jimmy started to cry.

"Shut up and enjoy," he said.

Jimmy laid helpless. *Where is my mom? Where are my brothers? No one appeared to be home. How is any of this possible? Where did everyone go?*

He finally released Jimmy and said if he told anyone, he would take him down. He also said he would hurt his mother or maybe they would find him in the pool.

Jimmy laid on the floor in the dark hallway, trembling, fear consuming every inch of his body. He laid weak, beaten, and scared of dying and scared of living all at the same time. Jimmy put his pants on and worked his way up the stairs to the bathroom near his bedroom.

Without notice, he was grabbed by the back of the neck as a wet towel crossed his face, pinching his nose as the pain screeched throughout the room. Then his shirt was lifted from his body like his head wasn't attached to it. Jimmy went to his room and crawled into bed. He was drained. His body was weak, his face sore as he laid still, abandoned, helpless, and unprotected.

The next day, Jimmy was hoping for a black eye in the mirror, only to find no marks.

Jimmy began crying as he sat on the toilet seat in fear as he thought about running away. He prayed, *God, why? Give me a sign. What do I do? Where do I hide? Why are you not here? Why did this man do those things to me?"*

Jimmy continued to ask himself, *Is this guy like a professional who beats and rapes little kids?*

Jimmy showered, trying to wash the pain away, only to find it was still there when he looked in the mirror. Tears began to fill his eyes, and his body began to tremble. He became sick as the dry heaves over the toilet bowl reminded him of drowning in the pool.

Jimmy thought, *This guy is crazy, and he's going to kill me.*

He showed up for breakfast as Jimmy could feel his eyes glaring. He put food on his plate and avoided eye contact and conversation with everyone. Fear had become power, and the power had become fear, and Jimmy could find no way out. Jimmy picked at his breakfast, only to have his mother tell him to eat his food. He did everything he could do not to throw it back up onto his plate.

Thoughts began to gather. Jimmy went to the garage. He checked the light switch. He checked the door handle on the door. He checked the floor and looked in the truck, only to find he had cleaned every surface. The listening devices had been removed. Any trace of the night appeared to be invisible, and Jimmy would become just a story. The blood on his face and shirt and anything he could say was washed away.

Jimmy found himself walking a new path, worn by traffic and lacking meaning or understanding of his next moves.

A few months later, Jimmy had gone to his girlfriend's house to visit as he would try to avoid home as much as possible. They had only kissed once, although Jimmy wasn't interested in anyone else and couldn't wait for that next kiss. Jimmy was learning about love and the kindness and care of another person.

Although she knew Jimmy was being beaten and they talked about everything, he never told her about being raped. Jimmy felt he was put in the position of protecting anyone and everyone he loved or cared about, as predicting this guy's next move was impossible and creepy beyond imagination.

They had talked about parents that hit their kids and how love or the action of love can be delivered in many ways. Although how can any parent hurt their children for any other reason other than making them afraid and fear them as a powerful person? Jimmy struggled privately with his emotions. His mind was riddled with shame and filled with whys.

Where is the father image, with guidance and protection?

Jimmy had wanted to go to the Dairy Queen, and his mother was working in the home office. He went to ask if they could go, and as he walked around the corner, he was there. Jimmy asked if she had time for a question. His stepdad's eyes filled with fire.

Jimmy began to tremble. He knew he was in trouble after seeing that look. He did it anyway. He said, "Mom, you're always working, and I want to go to my dad's."

His face, those eyes all became filled with a scary expression of attack. Jimmy left fast. He immediately went to the bathroom and turned to lock the door, although he was already there, grabbing Jimmy by the neck and lifting him from the ground as he pushed him against the glass shower door. Jimmy looked down as his feet left the ground. His fist began to close. Jimmy knew what was next as he wiggled, gasping for air, and he closed his eyes as he felt the force of his fist connecting with his face.

Jimmy's head shattered the glass shower door as he fell to the floor. He heard the glass hitting the floor behind him as he opened his eyes and was sitting in glass only to see him run from the bathroom doorway. Jimmy checked for blood, thinking this was it, he would have his chance. His mom would know everything that he had done to him, and it would be over.

Although Jimmy had renewed strength, his cry and tears were real and uncontrollable as he climbed up from the floor.

The shower door had relieved some of the hit to his face when the glass broke, and although Jimmy could feel no blood anywhere, he began checking in the mirror for cuts to his face or the back of his head. He met his mother at the top of the stairs, only to see him over her shoulder. His eyes were piercing at Jimmy.

Fear set in. Jimmy wanted to just say it: "he pulled my pants down and raped me," although before Jimmy could say a word, she told him to get ready for bed, and Jimmy knew his painful secret would have to wait. His mind filled with panic and worry as he recognized the beginning of another change in his everyday life.

As Jimmy walked back down the stairs, thinking this was not over, his mother thankfully followed him. He began to think she was bringing him to bed. No, she was only there to clean up the glass from the bathroom floor.

Jimmy was still thankful she was there because it kept him away from him.

Is she afraid of him too? Did he threaten her life?

Jimmy was thinking he knew the answers because although he knew his mother loved him, the biggest question that remained unknown was, Would he really kill us?

After Jimmy's mother finished cleaning up the glass, he heard the light switch in the bathroom and the hallway being turned off.

The house was silent, and it appeared that everyone was sleeping. Jimmy had to use the bathroom and, strangely, was interested in seeing the place where he once felt safe. When he entered the bathroom, it had new meaning, strange and disturbing. The door frame hung in its original position and appeared it would only need new glass. He sensed it would appear different even after the glass was replaced. Jimmy used the bathroom and began to return to his room. When he returned to his room, the feeling of vulnerability grabbed his attention. He became uneasy and thought about hiding or even running away. Right then, he was pushed from behind, hitting his brother's bed and falling to the floor. Jimmy's brother was at a sleepover, and Jimmy had the room to himself, although tonight, he wished his little brother was home.

The door closed. It was dark and silent. He was lifted to the bed, and Jimmy began to tremble, totally consumed by unhappiness as his face was again covered by his pillow. Jimmy's anticipation of what came next was as normal as flushing the toilet as he was hit several times. Jimmy laid there hoping, wishing, and praying for it to be over.

The pressure was lightening on his face, only to feel his pants being unzipped and pulled to his knees.

This terrible man did his miserable abuse again. Jimmy, from beneath the pillow, tears in his eyes, asked him to stop, "Please stop, please."

His only reply was "Tell me you like it."

Jimmy stayed still without saying a word. Even if he punched him again, Jimmy didn't care, and he would rather take the beating than resort to telling him what he wanted him to say. Jimmy wanted him to beat him up so badly that he would have to go to the hospital and then he would go to jail.

To Jimmy's surprise, the room remained quiet. No words, no sounds. He laid there waiting for him to be done.

Why did he like to beat up and have sex with little kids? Jimmy learned the man his mother had married was really a miserable man.

It appeared he was a person that evidently liked to physically beat and rape as a teaching method of controlling him with fear as it concealed his secret, and he was willing to kill for it, or at least threaten to kill for it.

Jimmy didn't know a lot about the sexual perversion of a person that prefers children as a sexual object, although he did discover later that his mother's husband spent a lot of time around gay men within his company and a few outside his circle.

Finally, he was done. He reminded Jimmy, "Not a word or you know what will happen." Jimmy had thoughts about calling the police, although he remembered the listening devices on the phone lines, and would they even believe him?

Would he say the kid has a brain injury and has mental health issues, or would he simply drown him in the swimming pool?

Jimmy lived in a world of fear. This man was someone who knew how to manipulate fear as a tool and used it as a control device for everyone and everything around him.

How do people learn or become this type of person?

He was learning there were people that hurt others and justified that it's acceptable behavior and shelter the behavior as their secret. They even threaten to kill for it.

In Jimmy's mind, it had become dark. The air he breathed carried the struggle to survive. He discovered holding on to everything he had left was requiring courage and determination as he searched for the unknown strengths within him. Jimmy continued to learn and discover more about the wrongs of people, the ability they have to abuse authority like it's free and without consequence.

How does one see mistreatment of others as normal behavior without seeing the destruction left behind?

At what point does someone threaten another's life to conceal the person they really are or have become?

We learn monsters don't really exist, although Jimmy had discovered some roam free, disguised as people, concealing the identity of who they really are. They are just that—monsters leaving paths of destruction as they move around. They develop a pattern to abuse someone that can't possibly protect themselves.

Jimmy had begun thinking of ways to get away from the monster. He began thinking like someone else, someone Jimmy didn't recognize. Someone ready to fight back.

CHAPTER 8

Interruption

It was 1973, and Jimmy had become a teenager.

Now at thirteen, lots of things began to change. Jimmy felt stronger and smarter. The milestone in his life appeared to have new meaning, and new beginnings, although unfortunately, new drama.

Jimmy noticed things had changed. He had become less interested in him. Fear became less within his thoughts, and happiness appeared simple again.

Jimmy was thankful, although untrusting. Confidence in his actions was not going to change anytime soon.

He made sure to keep a close eye on his little brother. He made sure that man was never alone with him. He would rather die than give him the chance to touch his little brother. He was identifying the fear that was controlling him for most of his life. He started to recap the things he was afraid of, the things holding him away from truly being happy. He wanted to know how to receive the sincere love and happiness of the beginning.

The fear of not being forgiven by his little brother had never changed. He also had the continued fear that friendships inside and outside of the family, when they had the knowledge of his brain injury or seizures, would judge him.

Jimmy's fear of emotional, physical, and sexual abuse, although concluded, remained a memory of the unfairness life can deliver. Jimmy's brain injury had made him weak or mentally unable to live life without that level of fear. Some classify it as paranoia, he discovered. The level of fear had been created by someone else's actions and continue to control his thoughts. Jimmy had the fear of acceptance as a person and would ask himself if he was deserving of any good in life. Maybe all these experiences had stripped away his ability to achieve his dreams and goals. Jimmy was hoping that the interruptions in his journey, or anyone's, could be changed and be redirected.

The joy and happiness that everyone dreams of can be held down like a brick in the water, where it sits on the bottom unless you find others to help lift the weight.

Jimmy's acceptance of circumstances and feeling deserving of any given thing or action had to be recognized.

It is said by many: we can be our own worst enemy.

Jimmy found any happiness to be temporary or in the moment. Although he realized many people have fears, secrets, or concealed memories, his appeared to be interrupting the very thought pattern to his happiness.

The gifts we are given at birth can become shadows when the secrets become more consuming than happiness and love for oneself. The feelings became a broken light switch that begins to turn off and on without control.

It's not a lonely place Jimmy had learned within his travels. Most have secrets that continue to control all walks of life. Even the doctors with good intentions who try to control the switch with unnecessary medications have secrets.

Jimmy's story is not about the hardships of life and the violations of others. It's about the possibilities of people around the world that find themselves sad, unhappy, or, yes, even depressed. If they could only remember God's got our back. He stands with us every day, no matter what kind of person we are or have become. People around the world can do great things. In most cases, they control their definition, although the ability to cheat, steal, and lie to retain secrets defines the person they will most likely become.

Now this is where it becomes interesting because we have all past by unhappiness. It's as normal as apple pie, although in many cases, intentional.

What is the personal gain or satisfaction of this intention?

As the winter thaw began, the sun became warmer, the snow melted from rooftops. The icicles hung from its edges as the water followed to the end of its journey and dripped to the ground with another new beginning.

As the ice melted from lakes, and Jimmy's water ski season approached, summer began to appear again.

Jimmy was so excited about this year's competitions. When he was on the water, it was like the world turned off and it was just him and his ski, gliding across the glass-covered lake. He often thought there was nothing better, nothing happier, nothing cooler than standing on water.

Jimmy had several competitions with wins this year and satisfied the requirements to ski in the regional competition at a lake just outside of Des Moines, Iowa.

He would have to place as one of the top three to go to the national competition in Petersburg, Virginia. He had trained hard this year and had the determination to become a champion in his division.

It was a warm day in Iowa, and although the heat of summer was ending, the winds of fall weather were beginning to pick up.

Depending on the size of the lake, it can be just a little rough. Jimmy would need to adjust throughout, completing the course. He knew his competition would be very good, and butterflies soon set in as he waited for his turn to ski. This would be Jimmy's biggest opportunity as a professional athlete in the water ski association, and the possibilities became a little overwhelming.

This was it. This was what all the training and competition had delivered, and soon Jimmy could be a national champion and on his way to the possibility of a world champion one day. Jimmy's name was called to the starting dock, and hearing his name announced added inspiration. As he sat on the dock, placing his foot in the boot, he set his ski down on the water and felt fear gaining strength. He quickly focused on the rope, the boat and the judge towers flanking the course. He began anticipating a good run and gave the tow boat the nod and said, "Hit it."

Jimmy was soon setting up for his approach, cutting across the wake around the first ball as he headed for the second, and finally completed the six-ball course.

The second run was completed at a faster speed, and the boat stopped as the rope was shortened fifteen feet.

This would give Jimmy a short time to rest, although to be fair, to each skier, it was done as quickly as possible and then back up on the water. The boat wake was a little different than Jimmy usually skied behind, although his ability made up for the difference, and as he set his approach, he could feel the win.

As he rounded the first ball and across the wake for the second, he had to reach a little further because of the shorter rope, and although he was able to round the second ball, he lost the rope. Jimmy found himself under the water. As he surfaced, he raised his hands to let the towboat know he was okay. The good news—Jimmy ended in first place. He was on the way to the national ski competition in Petersburg, Virginia. Jimmy would ski against the best in the country. He thought this just might be the happiest day of his life. The only problem was Jimmy needed to train, and the season had ended. With some luck, he was able to get enrolled at a training camp and would be leaving as soon as possible.

While making new friends attending the competition, Jimmy had met someone there that had a ski school in Florida. It would be nice and warm and all the ski time Jimmy could ever want or need.

Jimmy soon found himself in unfamiliar territory. Things seemed to be fun, full of joy, and happier than he could ever remember. The challenge suddenly became worrying how to hang on to the rope rather than how to hold on to life. The ski school in Florida became the win, and training with regional champions from throughout the country had become the dream Jimmy had worked so hard to achieve.

Can dreams that come true be by design?

It was truly an honor for him, and skiing there for the next two weeks, six times a day, had become one of Jimmy's greatest achievements.

Although it did come with painful arms and legs. Even his hands, if he didn't know better, would scream at him when he removed his gloves. The memories of this experience would last a lifetime.

After Jimmy finished training in Florida, he would have an even bigger opportunity to ski with two national champions in North Carolina.

What was happening was like the floodgates were open, and the water was pouring in. Jimmy was having the time of his life.

The opportunity to meet and ski with two people on their way to becoming second-time national champions was nothing short of amazing.

The hope and love he had for himself created a path, and even though Jimmy knew this may be a once-in-a-lifetime opportunity, the path was clear, new, and untouched. What Jimmy realized and learned was that people experience things in our lifetime that become bits and pieces of time within the minutes of our journey.

Jimmy traveled the following week with his fellow athletes to Petersburg, Virginia. His family would be meeting up with him, and Jimmy knew he would be there. After being far away from home, free and happy, without thought and after becoming a chick magnet, the excitement Jimmy should have become a little faded. Although he hadn't seen his family for almost a month, he wasn't looking forward to seeing them. The reminder of the abuse soon began to control and reenter Jimmy's arena.

Jimmy recognized the muddy waters and began instantly making the attempt to clear his mind.

He fought with the crap he thought was history but remained a secret.

Quickly he was reminded of the pain of physical abuse. It appeared to be planted like a tree, where the roots continue to spread throughout the ground even after the tree is cut down. This would be Jimmy's biggest competition, and he could be a national champion by the end of the weekend. He liked where his mind was and wanted it to never end. His time spent here would be the memories that he would cherish and hold as treasures. Jimmy was reminded of his promise, the promise of happiness, love, and hope that fill dreams.

Can minutes of the journey be removed from time?

When Jimmy arrived, his family was already there. He was excited to see them and then what he had expected became real. He was there.

Jimmy didn't even want to say hi to him and avoided the opportunity. He tried hard to focus on the competition and remain in his happy place as he reviewed the lake and mentally prepared for the trip across its waters.

The next morning, as Jimmy sat on the dock, waiting for the towboat to prepare for the course, his thoughts appeared clear and untainted.

The handle of the rope began to tighten in his hands as he looked at the lake that was man-made and overfilled to allow all three events.

Jimmy had noticed the power poles in the lake were wrapped with bed mattress to protect the slalom skiers from hitting the poles the day before, although when the time came, an added little touch of fear was unavoidable.

Jimmy said to himself, *Shake it off, Jimmy, shake it off.*

The rope began to tighten as it lifted from the water. Jimmy nodded and said, "Hit it."

Jimmy's ski was feeling good as he prepared for his approach. The water was smooth like glass. The bright-orange balls reflected their color off the surface of the water and began to call his name. It was simply amazing, although Jimmy's mind began to wonder as he cut across the wake around the first ball and across to the second.

Spectators stood watching on the shoreline, and Jimmy enjoyed the feeling of being very important and the possibility of that championship title.

Jimmy suddenly slipped back into his head. His thoughts became overwhelming as the flashes and images began to take over his concentration. There were no second chances at this course. One time only, and there was no turning around to regroup and get his head back in the game.

What's happening?

Jimmy turned around the second ball and then the pole with the bed mattress wrapped around its trunk was in his vision, and that's all it took. That single image completely destroyed Jimmy's concentration, and into the water he went. This would not be Jimmy's year. As he lost the rope when he hit the wake with a bad edge and fell into the water, he decided to stay under for enough time to be disappointed. His head came to the surface, and he raised his arms as he began feeling sad about all the training and practice. Jimmy started to wonder if he just wasn't good enough to even be in the competition, although he was quickly reminded, *He is there!*

Jimmy thought to himself, *What was the distraction trigger that reopened the past?*

The next day, Jimmy and his family had started home, and although he was heartbroken about the competition, his thoughts contained the great times getting there.

Even with the embarrassment in front all of his fellow athletes, Jimmy held on to those memories and continued to hold those memories as some of his life's most important and valued lessons. He had the greatest respect for the people he had worked with and those that went on to be world champions.

Jimmy's emotions just wanted to blow up, and he wanted to tell his family all the things going through his mind out there on the water. His family had traveled far to support him in his efforts. They were happy for him, excited for him, and he had let them down. More importantly, he had let himself down. Jimmy had let the tragedies in his life take one of his biggest opportunities and trashed it, all because he didn't take care of himself, and fear won the game again.

Jimmy knew he would be home soon, and this unleashed a little anxiety because although he identified the things keeping him afraid, it didn't make them go away.

Jimmy had stubbornly struggled, thinking the past was the past and couldn't hurt him anymore. He was learning the opposite was true.

The things that controlled Jimmy would never let go, it seemed. They held on, fighting for survival within himself. They continued to control his thoughts of anger and fear and his ability to become better and grow.

He was damaged, no longer in perfect condition. The need for fresh water to run through Jimmy's creek had become noticeable. The smoothing and polishing of the rocks that lie on its bottom became smudged although its shores began to splash the promise of better days for tomorrow.

Why is no longer being in perfect condition so hard to admit?

Most say denial is the enemy. To admit the truth with one's self is the challenge, and the courage to accept the challenge becomes the problem. Jimmy had learned very early at the age of eight that he was no longer in perfect health and was mentally challenged by the fact he was no longer perfect.

What do I look like? What do I talk like? Can they tell, and if so, why does it matter?

CHAPTER 9

Embracing

The school year had started, and things were going well for Jimmy. Fifteen was just around the corner, and he decided to run for the president of the yearbook committee. Jimmy found himself very popular with people and the girls.

When he joined the basketball team, that became his new passion. Although it demanded hard work and a lot of running, his determination and strength came in every step.

He wasn't always the best shot, although he could run five miles a day, and the endurance to move the ball made up for the lack of shots on the hoop. Jimmy even had the dream of going pro one day, although the coach squashed the thought.

"You're not tall enough."

Again, he found himself a little disappointed.

Jimmy stood next to the measuring stick on the wall, and it confirmed he reached six feet two inches.

Jimmy believed he was tall enough. Little did he realize at the time that college draft picks were generally six-foot-four-inch minimums, unless you can make three-point shots behind your back.

Jimmy did continue to play the game, as it was fun, and it didn't hurt his popularity. He also did become the leader of the yearbook committee and learned a lot from the experience as a person in a leadership role. The plus for Jimmy was that his favorite friend was on the committee. She was fun, well-liked, and was a great addition to the group.

Jimmy's homelife had improved, and his mother had become distant from her husband, and he would be leaving soon. This wasn't bad news for Jimmy as it would close a door on the horrible chapter of his life where fear and disappointment became his only image. Interestingly to Jimmy, he avoided being around the house as much as possible and seemed very awkward and almost nervous to be there. The day couldn't come fast enough as far as Jimmy was concerned, and maybe the family would embrace the day he left.

Jimmy didn't express how happy he was to his mother.

He didn't know how she felt about his departure or any other feelings she may have about who he was as a person, and his mothers' feelings were very important to him. The question was, would she feel relieved after he was gone?

Then there he was, standing in Jimmy's bedroom doorway with that horrifying look on his face. Jimmy didn't want to get beaten up again, although he wasn't going down without a fight and told him, "Leave."

The next words didn't come with surprise.

"If you say anything, I will take you down and finish you."

Before Jimmy could blink, he was gone.

The following week, his mother told Jimmy and his brothers and sister he was gone and would not be coming back.

Jimmy wanted to jump up and down with joy, although surprisingly, his mom seemed sad about his departure. He stood in disbelief, not understanding how she could even think twice about him leaving. The things he had done didn't leave much room for any feelings except relief.

Jimmy wanted to tell his mother he had threatened him on the way out the door, although he wasn't sure if she was still in contact with him. He decided to not take the chance.

Months later, when the school year was ending, Jimmy's mother had found a new job. She became very busy, and although she made the attempt to continue water skiing for the family, it became a memory.

It was another seizure-free year for Jimmy, and the doctors approved the possibility of Jimmy discontinuing his medications. This would give him the ability to start driver's education and actually receive a driver's license. He had worried about the possibility of not having the ability to drive. That was a valid possibility.

Is the believing in you the key to unused wealth?

Jimmy slowly weaned himself off medications without any problems and did receive his license after a year of remaining seizure-free without them. The excitement became more than most. With this new opportunity, he felt a little more like everybody else. He still avoided the brain injury topic, and it would continue to remain one of his well-kept secrets. At this point, Jimmy felt it was his business. If he were to get sick, well, they would just know.

The thought of others knowing about his brain injury had always remained threatening, and he didn't want people to treat him differently or have it unfairly steal any good opportunities.

Over the years, Jimmy had to learn to accept the small lesion on the back of his brain that caused seizures.

The hard part was growing up without letting it define him as a person. Brain injuries don't get better; they tend to worsen over time and would remain the anchor in his life's travels. Jimmy sheltered his condition to protect his chances of opportunity, without judgment of whether he could complete the task.

The judgment and mistreatment over time had proven people, with intention or not, had reservations dealing with others that struggle from any type of head injury.

Jimmy never let his head injury hold back his drive for success, although the emotional consequences seemed to keep him from ever having complete and true happiness.

Through Jimmy's determination, and obviously challenging times, he would hear others talk about people with similar injuries. He found most a little disturbing.

Their judgments or conclusions in many cases were hurtful.

The world lives in a place where people continue to be very misguided. They tend to believe head injuries, along with epilepsy, should be placed in one category and the possibilities within their future become limited by unfair judgement.

In Jimmy's case, visible signs can be heavily covered. Others may have disfigurement, speech impairments, and possible balance problems.

It confirmed the complete misunderstanding of damage to a very important component of the body. Jimmy had found through experiences that others quickly make hurtful judgments. In many cases, people with brain injuries are far from their expectations and regularly described as crazy people without thought and placed on the list of people that should be ignored.

Jimmy's mom bought him a car after he received his license. It wasn't much, but it was his. It was small and white, had no fenders, but thirty miles to the gallon was the best part, as gas was ¢45 a gallon, and money was tight.

CHAPTER 10

Wondering

It was 1977. Jimmy had just turned seventeen and was having a blast in high school. He did try but wasn't the most engaged student, although popular with many friends. He enjoyed being on the yearbook committee, and as a leader in the past, the many responsibilities would give him the opportunity to use them as tools in his future.

As Jimmy worked his way through the many challenges over the years, it appeared his skies just may be lifting.

He could feel the wind in his sail, and his tiny boat had become larger as it began carrying him to better waters.

Jimmy felt safe, happy, filled with new energy.

Another year without medications and seizures had delivered a little extra excitement this year and filled him with joy and inspiration.

The feeling of sharing inspiration became part of Jimmy's mind-set. He began studying the very content of being inspired about life, about friendships, and about the possibilities tomorrow could bring.

Jimmy's primary focuses on inspiration were about the possibility of helping others with the use of positive communication and body language. He already had some experience with finding ways to bring happiness to others with simple words. He knew how that felt firsthand and wanted to share it with others. True happiness can be expressed through laughter and, yes, tears, through passion and excitement. Not unlike the first kick in your mother's belly, where you were unable to see your future, although you couldn't wait to get out there and explore the possibilities. Jimmy had discovered that most people became the happiest when talking about their personal interests and achievements. He quickly recognized the joy in their words, the inspiration within their body language, and the reinforcement within their journey.

The possibilities to inspire someone has no ending.

Jimmy was at that age now where choices lead to challenging and thoughtful consideration. As a group of Jimmy's friends gathered around the campfire one night, he made a choice to try his first beer. It didn't taste great, although he finished the can so others wouldn't make fun of him. Let's just say Jimmy ended up holding on to a tree when the beer returned for the second taste and decided maybe drinking wasn't his thing. Unfortunately, he had also made a choice to try some marijuana and, shortly after, found himself in trouble. Although Jimmy was still very young, he was a little disappointed with himself, and he chose to seek counseling.

His mother had made him an appointment, and he had very little idea what to expect. He thought maybe he would get a lecture or something like that.

When Jimmy arrived at the clinic, it looked like a hospital. It had big black glass walls, was five stories tall, and surrounded by green trees and landscape. His mother had driven, and as she parked the car, all Jimmy could say was, "Wow, there sure are a lot of people with problems."

As Jimmy entered the building, he had taken notice of the black marble floors and all-black furniture filling the lobby. The walls were gray with black-painted door frames, and all seemed a little dark for inspirational conversations.

Jimmy began wondering about how people must feel when entering. He already lacked inspiration about the appointment and now found himself in a room lined by darkness. Jimmy sat quietly, waiting for his turn in the lobby, when the counselor introduced himself, and thankfully, he wasn't wearing black clothes. The walk down the hallway to his office seemed long and almost never-ending. As Jimmy sat down, he was asked what he wanted to talk about.

Jimmy replied, "I don't know."

The counselor then suggested to start with why you like to smoke pot.

As Jimmy looked out the window, he said, "It's really no big deal."

After they talked for a while, it appeared Jimmy was struggling with his childhood abuse issues as they remained unresolved and without conclusion.

Jimmy began to think about the unfinished issues. Determining maybe this chair, the one he found himself in at this very moment, was where he was supposed to be.

Just maybe, this was Jimmy's opportunity to clear the way, to open new doors, to be all he could be or all he wanted to be.

The counselor looked at Jimmy with interest and said "let's get started" as he took him to another room. Soon another counselor entered the room and, without words, placed a game in front of Jimmy. His first impression was a little uncomfortable as he wondered if he would be talking with a woman about being beaten up and sexually abused. He became a little distracted by her beauty as she said hello and continued to dump all the blocks of the game on the table.

She instructed him to put the round block in the round hole and the square block in the square hole. Jimmy blurted out, "You have to be kidding me, I'm seventeen."

She looked at Jimmy with a smile, appeared to be well aware of his age, and simply said "do it" and left the room. Jimmy sat still for a few minutes as he attempted to understand the reason for this process. He soon found himself wondering about his brain injury, thinking maybe they think he's stupid or something. He suddenly became inspired, and he was going to show them. He began putting the round blocks into the round holes and the square blocks into the square holes. After completing the game, he did feel a little stupid. Lucky for Jimmy, the blocks were colored red and blue.

The room was very quiet now, and he became aware of how narrow the windows were. Jimmy soon found himself looking at the beautiful trees and the landscape that surrounded the building and wondering what could be next. Then she returned and walked into the room. She told him "good job" and dumped the blocks back on the table again and said "do it again" and left the room.

Jimmy was very confused and really wondering about this whole counseling thing.

He put all the blocks in the holes again and was getting irritated. When she returned, he was going to ask her if they would be talking at some point.

The counselor reentered the room, told him he did a good job, and told him that was it for today.

Jimmy quickly stood up and left the room very confused, again asking himself, *What just happened?*

Jimmy returned to the front where his mother was waiting. He was feeling a little drained and affected by the embarrassment, as the shame and humiliation of his long-ago childhood was no longer a secret.

He did not want to continue this process but fully understood it was not an option.

Everyone was very nice to Jimmy, although they looked at him differently than when he came in. Not judgmental, and possibly with the tint of compassion.

He still wasn't sure what was happening, but were they seeing physical and sexual abuse or his brain injury or all three.

Jimmy heard his mother making additional appointments. He began feeling uncomfortable, and he motioned his mother to the front door.

His only hope was they had talked with his mother about the challenges he was facing. The whole way home, there was no conversation, no apology, no justification, no admission of error, and certainly no expression of regret.

Jimmy continued to feel a little numb by the experience, and as he watched the world go by down the roadway, he thought about how she must feel.

Did she think it was acceptable punishment? Did she feel the way Jimmy expected?

Jimmy loved his mother, and although frustrated, angered, and confused, he held back, just wanting to scream out loud,

"He beat me up, Mom, why didn't you stop him?"

"He raped me, Mom."

"Were you afraid? Did he threaten to kill you too?"

"I'm waiting, Mom, tell me how you feel."

Jimmy felt fear, controlling fear, the manipulated fear that blocked any peace.

Jimmy's mind continued to climb like a roller coaster. As it rolled over the top and down the steep glide to the bottom, the car slowed to a stop. He struggled to communicate his frustration, finding ways within him to inspire positive communication, judgment, and any anger at his mother.

Why is he still controlling her? Why is he still controlling me?

Jimmy was reminded of the pain throughout events as he attempted to work through them all, with little success on his own. His experiences were kept hidden as he grew with many unspoken words.

Through Jimmy's determination, he was learning to go beyond the self-judgment. He pushed forward and hoped to work through unfinished business as he attended his next counseling visit.

Although he unexpectedly found himself putting blocks in the holes again, two months and eight visits later, Jimmy had enough of the block thing and was ready to express his feelings.

At his next counseling visit, there came some surprises as he mentioned he had enough of the blocks and didn't want to do them anymore. The counselor looked at Jimmy with a smile on her face and said, "Good, now let's get to work."

Jimmy still didn't understand why she made him do the blocks, although he believed it was about to be discussed.

Jimmy had completed many exercises and discussions over the next four months and although the memories would always be with him as the trauma of abuse could be felt for a lifetime, Jimmy felt free of its torment. It helped him better understand why people hurt others in this manner and the destruction it leaves behind. The counselors were helping Jimmy be aware that the dents and bruises will never go away, but he could continue to live as a survivor rather than a victim. That was the path of success in recovery. He was learning the importance of working through the emotional issues of being abused.

He learned in many cases the behavior can be ingrained as acceptable or okay.

A cycle that repeats itself. A cycle that can continue for generations if not stopped in its tracks.

Jimmy had learned about the damage left behind when forgiveness seemed unlikely. Yet new strengths were being found. The joy, the love, and the happiness became a clear goal as Jimmy moved on through the counseling sessions.

Jimmy had met a new girlfriend not long after and she was fun and filled with energy and they did everything together. Their relationship was well-known, and after graduation, Jimmy even thought about them moving in together. He had found a nice small house and signed the lease.

The relationship was good, and the happiness they shared together went on for some time. Jimmy had researched new employment with temporary relocation in Texas, and this would not come without a challenge for him. He was in love. Although discussion of her relocating with him was possible, he knew in his heart she would never make the move.

Jimmy had gone to check out the position and housing located nearby the place where he would be working. Sadly, he found the place to be a little rough and very small, and it had very little to offer for either housing or employment. Jimmy concluded the move would not be a good fit. A move was not in the plan. He would research other employment opportunities locally.

But while he was away, she found herself in love with someone else, and they were going to get married.

Jimmy had deep feelings for her, and as disappointed as he was, he understood that distance between two people that care for each other can leave a hole for loneliness and the bandage can be complicated.

Jimmy was very happy for her, as she was one of his best friends. Although the newly formed relationship was difficult, they remained good friends.

CHAPTER 11

Difficulty

In the spring of 1980, Jimmy began working as a laborer and had interest in becoming a carpenter. He had started school at a technical college in the field of carpentry, although the job placement was poor. After completing his first year, Jimmy changed to floor covering for an immediate position with a local company.

When Jimmy graduated from tech school, he decided to start a company primarily engaged in the multifamily industry, where he would deliver full-service floor covering needs to local and national property investment groups.

While visiting a local floor covering company, Jimmy met the woman he would marry. She was bright, hardworking, stunningly beautiful, and tall, just like Jimmy. They were engaged a short time later, and Jimmy wanted to make sure she understood he had a brain injury, and it might be possible for him to have a seizure.

In most cases, seizures do not cause death, although for the person having them, it's like you die and come back to life, waiting for the next one to happen.

Jimmy, although thankful for the few seizures he had, recognized the challenge for those who face seizures every day.

The journey of the day can be filled with unknowns, dead and reborn only to have the same experience within a few hours or a few tomorrows.

Jimmy had been off medication for nine years and seizure-free for thirteen years and began each day hoping for the best. But now he found himself about to have the scariest conversation in his life. Although she was his new best friend and their relationship was happy, full of life and love, judgment and rejection will remain an option.

Jimmy wouldn't have it any other way, and he fully understood the possibility that she would decline his proposal.

The happiness and love he had for her went beyond his own wants or needs, and he recognized the importance of her love and happiness. It was just a chance he would have to take.

One of Jimmy's biggest fears in life was when anyone would have to care for him when he had one of his seizures. When he would awake from a seizure, the room would always be very quiet, as those present would appear to be stunned or maybe overwhelmed by witnessing the experience.

At times he would wonder about his ability to hear and see directly afterward. Jimmy found interest in his recoveries, as it would appear the lights would go out, and the brain would take a short period of time to reboot. He always tried to explain to anyone present during the episode to help ease their emotional impact.

Jimmy knew in his heart living with and understanding their love and happiness would be challenged.

There was always the possibility of a helpless feeling a person might have when one of these episodes happens to someone. Also, the memory that remains like residue.

Often, Jimmy had thoughts about others with epilepsy or seizure disorders.

People can have one or many seizures in any given day.

He always related to their pain and their disappointment. He hoped they had prayer to surround them with comfort, care, and love. Jimmy's experiences with seizures were few in his lifetime. He also fully understood the possibility of sharing his condition with her may have some questions or concerns with challenge. After their short discussion, Jimmy popped the question. With teary eyes and the expression of happiness on her face, she said, "Yes, I will marry you!"

They then decided to call her parents and have the next big conversation. They arrived with joined hands and entered the house with smiles. Jimmy wasted no time and asked for the hand of their daughter in marriage as he could see their anxious anticipation with the call to come over and meet with them.

Jimmy found himself a little intimidated due to the fact that they were both very young, and he didn't have a lot to offer at the time. He tried hard to convey that his love, hope, and happiness he had for their daughter would always come first and it would never waver.

With some understandable concern, they were given the blessing they both had come for and were married the following year.

In 1983, Jimmy had learned his longtime friend had experienced a seizure and, after some time, was diagnosed with epilepsy. She began taking medication like Jimmy, and he called to express how he felt about the news and that if she ever wanted to talk about it, he was there for her.

This was the person mentioned earlier in the story as Jimmy's first kiss, and after many years, their friendship had remained special, and their close friendship never weakened.

They had the kind of friendship that carried a special bond. That kind of person that walks into your life for a reason unknown at the time, although your connection becomes implanted within your heart and mind.

The kind of friend that everyone needs, although many live without or simply miss its opportunity. The one that shares life's most difficult times without judgments.

When disappointments continued to fill daily life, Jimmy had discovered someone that could help him better understand the power in its definition.

Strangely, this unique friend in Jimmy's life now shares the same condition and challenges. Jimmy and his wife gathered regularly with her and her husband. The conversation of seizures was rarely discussed, yet Jimmy and his friend shared something they both could do without. She was having seizures on a regular basis, and although she was on medication, she lived in that space of fear of the unknown, and Jimmy related to her concerns. Seizures for her had unknown circumstance, and this is common with epilepsy, although becoming afraid of tomorrow becomes the most unfair experience in life.

It becomes life without the guarantee of tomorrow and questions hopes, dreams, and promise.

The good news is the suffering that accompanies it doesn't destroy one's faith; it refines its existence. Jimmy was soon challenged emotionally, physically, and mentally regarding something he had always avoided thoughts about—he received the call informing him his best friend in the world had died. She had a seizure while she was alone holding her newborn baby in her arms, and after swallowing her tongue, she suffocated before the episode was over.

She was thirty-seven and filled with happiness and joy. The kind where her laughter filled the room and others felt the joy.

Jimmy's faith became challenged. God had become absent, and he cried with anger as the experience of her death became real and was compounded by the clear understanding of why it happened. He had spoken to her two days before her death. She had mentioned her tiredness and weakness. As Jimmy hugged her goodbye, she expressed concern about the way she was feeling, and he told her to get some rest.

She had been breastfeeding and very fatigued from lack of sleep. Jimmy knew she had discontinued her medication to allow her to breastfeed, and he was very uncomfortable with her choice because of her condition.

Jimmy had thought about contacting her sister and letting her know how dangerous it was for her. He was concerned, and she needed help to get the badly needed rest to avoid a possible seizure.

Again, Jimmy would experience the consequence of choice, the one phone call that could have possibly saved his best friend's life. She died holding her baby girl as she was breastfeeding, lying down on the couch in her family room.

This new mother had unknowingly given the ultimate sacrifice. To give her child everything, happiness and love and care for the healthiest start in life she could possibly give her. Jimmy knew his best friend well, and she wouldn't have it any other way.

As her family struggled with her death, Jimmy observed the heartbreak related to seizures, where the unknown and the unfairness take away the young and, in this case, the mother of two.

Death comes in so many shapes and sizes. The lack of understanding seizures that rarely kill you becomes the dark and unknown mystery. Jimmy would best describe it as a brain attack.

Jimmy had struggled for some time with fear of the unknown, the fear of when his final day will come, although he lives each day making every effort to be happy, even when it can be annoying for someone when they could possibly be having a bad day. He struggles and tries as hard as possible to recognize or pay attention to people's moods, although falls short from time to time without intention. He is in no hurry, of course, to get there but is comforted by the belief that they will see each other again someday.

The reality is, what comes after death is unknown, but Jimmy would like to believe every child experiences many different journeys within many different lives. As we return to the beginning, we all die as one gift and one life.

He would like to believe it starts with a smile and a hug.

Christmas 1985 holiday season was fast approaching with shopping, food, and lots of candy in its future. Jimmy was excited for the days away from work, but spending time with family has always been the star at the top of the tree. Some family members had called to go shopping, and Jimmy and his wife decided to go along. They met at Jimmy's sister's house and were going to have dinner first. Jimmy looked at the bowl of candy on the counter and decided he should have a piece before they headed out.

Unfortunately, the candy became stuck in Jimmy's throat, and after some attempts, he was down. Jimmy's brother-in-law began working hard to remove the candy, and as it popped out, rolling across the floor, that would be the last thing Jimmy remembered as he had a seizure.

As Jimmy came to, it was like other times, except that he felt terribly sick and went to the sink. As family stood behind him to keep him safe, his level of humiliation had taken a new horizon. Jimmy began apologizing for his illness to no one in particular. The sound of silence became noticeable, and Jimmy turned around to find a room filled by family and the paramedics waiting for him to be comfortable. This was not the first experience for his family, but it was the first for his wife. It was unpleasant—the best way to describe it. The brain short-circuits, the eye nerves pull to the forehead, the body becomes stiff with uncontrollable convulsions, or, in simple terms, the body shakes until the episode is over.

The recovery time varies depending on the severity of the episode, leaving the only response of rolling the person to their side to insure they will not swallow their tongue and suffocate.

Jimmy has always felt horrible as he recovers and sees the people caring for him. His biggest concern this time was for his wife to see what he had warned her about and hoped would never happen. The fear of this episode became real and would remain in her memory. He didn't say anything about how he was feeling at the time as he was frightened about their future together.

Would her hand slip away or simply let go? Could their love and courage pull them through?

Jimmy's seizure came with great disappointment, accompanied by sadness and humiliation. His wife and their families now had greater understanding of the severity of convulsive disorder, where helplessness, panic, and worry became a reality until the episode was over.

Jimmy also began to worry about his relationship with his wife. The fear that was absent from his mind for many years had returned. He was rudely reminded of the damage that would never go away.

It would continue to grow like ugly weeds in a beautiful flower garden that was supposed to hold peace and comfort.

The feeling of being different than others appeared to be back, and now he would most likely have to begin the medication regimen once more.

He also began to realize the list of triggers had become larger as the lack of oxygen appeared to have new meaning and was something to be considered on the list for survival.

He wondered if this would be too big of a challenge for her, as she observed the violent nature of seizures and the new form of fear entering her life.

Will *she want someone different? Will she still love me without feeling I am a burden?*

Jimmy's mind began to fill with thought of regret, and he asked himself if God was real, how could life be so full of the clutter of serious and disastrous problems. With the death of their friend, how will Jimmy's wife ever believe her husband won't die the same tragic way?

A few months had passed, and Jimmy's wife appeared to be understanding, and not much was discussed about it after some time.

Jimmy returned to his medication regimen. The excitement of gatherings where drinks, dancing, and laughter can be found had changed. Although Jimmy loved to dance and the enjoyment of the social activity, remained exciting. That could be a plus side though.

Jimmy had never known if there was enjoyment in drinking but wished he had the opportunity to choose whether or not to do it himself. Since the feeling of enjoyment from it was never going to be experienced, he didn't want it to limit his social life.

In 1991, Jimmy had a son, and his heart became filled by happiness. He always wanted a family so he could teach the next generation the art of kindness to others.

To his surprise, the baby slept many times through the night, although he became hungry in the earlier hours of the morning. He was a healthy young boy with a strong grip and appeared to have no problem speaking out.

Jimmy sure wished he could use his words rather than screams of wants and needs. He had the determination to be the best dad he could be, the dad he rarely had.

Jimmy wanted to be the dad that would be there for the achievements and the accomplishments, along with the disappointments.

Sometimes a child just needs his dad for support, promising everything will be fine, even though he knows life will have its turns and twists. He wanted to inspire happiness, love, hope, and protection.

Oftentimes, Jimmy would just watch him sleep as he would see an occasional smile as sweet dreams passed his way.

Jimmy was reminded of his first days as a free boy, ready to walk life's path with daily falls and rises to the unknown destinations and mysteries that were ahead. The comforts of God's gifts were safe within his mother's body, where education and the fear only for survival and happiness coexisted. It was a place where the love and compassion for others appeared within him, banked for another day to be shared freely.

Jimmy generally worked long days and sometimes only kissed his family goodbye in the morning before they were awake and kissed them good night after they were already asleep. He tried very hard to be there for his family, although he was addicted to his work. Jimmy always felt the need to make up for his disability and felt challenged each day as work and medications collided. He felt it fought so much of what he had to offer. He never wanted his family to want or need anything they didn't already have. He wanted them to feel safe and loved and cherished.

Jimmy wanted his son to be proud of his parents. He would give more of himself than he ever had. He also knew parents generally fall short most of the time as the energy left at the end of the day can be weak. Jimmy recognized the importance of care and understanding that become the valuable lessons children need in the early days of life and as they grow into adulthood. He was comforted by the recognition of his weakness and remained confident he would meet the challenge, and somehow, he would be there for his family.

Family—what an exciting word.

Jimmy loved his parents, although he just always wanted them to share more of their love, caring, and kindness he knew they both had.

Life's greatest gift, with life's greatest challenge, would surely be life's greatest achievement, and he had a commitment to accomplish this very precious goal.

It would become his roof without holes, protected from the rain, snow, and ice, as it becomes the victory.

When he was with his family and accepting their love, Jimmy could throw away the ugly and be filled with hope, gratefulness, happiness, and care.

In 1992, Jimmy and his wife were informed their son had a disability. He had apparently developed it shortly after he turned twelve months old. It was an immune system disorder, where the loss of hair, skin irritations, and painful fingernails became his challenge.

With very little understanding of how it would impact their child's life, they began to work through the fears of what was next. Jimmy's world had become small again, and God's promise became hard to grasp as Jimmy became closed-minded.

He was grateful his son was healthy in every other way, although the challenge of being different was in his future.

Learning about being a father for the first time came with challenges all by itself, although fear had begun to set in, and it became a little unmanageable. The love for his child soon became filled with tears, and the unknown became overwhelming.

Jimmy and his wife began bringing their son to every hospital and every doctor they could find who specialized in this field. Searching became almost like a full-time job. Protection mode kicked in, and emotions continued to run in high gear. Then one day, to their surprise, the doctor looked at them and said the words that would terrify any parent.

"There is nothing available that will help your son."

Jimmy and his wife loved their son more than life itself. He was perfect to them in every way, and they would take on the challenge with the help of children sharing the same condition from around the world. The learning process became difficult as their son became judged and mistreated by others the same way he was when he started school. The memories of how it felt to be different than others recreated the environment Jimmy once lived in.

Jimmy could tell his son felt very different than the other kids as he walked in the classroom. The excitement that most kids should have deflated like a balloon when it loses its air, as others moved away from him and stared at him with unknown conclusions. Jimmy clearly understood and felt the heartbreak of his first day in kindergarten as the room became silent and the other kids began to stare, lacking understanding of a condition where the hair simply vanishes without a trace and without a choice.

When he got off the bus crying, Jimmy and his wife knew quickly he was teased for being different.

His first words were, "They could see my brains, and I looked like a freak."

Jimmy talked with his son about kids just saying mean things because sometimes they just don't understand why someone is different. "To help them understand, let them know you can't help it and wish you had hair just like them, and soon you will find that some-one will like you just the way you are, and before long, you will have many new friends. You'll see, just give them a chance."

Like most kids, Jimmy's son said he was never going back to school ever again. Jimmy and his wife talked about it after he was in bed, and after, they shed some tears from feeling helpless. They decided maybe he could stay home, and they would visit the school and help the teachers guide them through the process.

To their surprise, the next morning, he was telling Jimmy to hurry up as he was going to miss the bus. Jimmy and his wife stood in amazement. "You're right, let's get going."

Smiles filled the room as they hurried out the door.

They did talk with the teachers, and they decided they would talk about the condition openly when he was ready, and the class could ask questions.

Time passed, and as their son grew older, he became stronger and had many friends. As judgment and mistreatment continued for several years, it had made their son emotionally stronger about his disability. Although still sensitive at times, the wonders of hair never escaped his dreams and hopes of having it one day.

Their son made it through the many tough days of judgment, staring, and conclusion. As children grow up and wish things were different, they many times conclude things may never change. They watched as their son shared it with his family and others each day. Jimmy found, being challenged by disability himself, it would be a part of his life.

Yes, life does deal cards of unfairness, but why should it become the everyday challenge? That was the giant question that would remain in Jimmy's mind.

Why do people treat others without kindness?

In Jimmy's career, he had the opportunity to work in housing where people lived with disability, obesity, and even circumstances created by the opportunity to serve our country. Jimmy learned that most do not share the mountain of pain with just anybody, and although that is okay in most cases, he believed every day was new and could be filled with adventure, mystery, and opportunity.

Recognizing opportunity—two words, one thought.

As most work through the challenge of being accepted as they are, with the courage, honor, and love for themselves, they continue to lack the ability to accept that someone somewhere would ever love them. Jimmy found the inability to fight the unfairness and the mistreatment of others adds to the vulnerability of any given situation and is carelessly overlooked by many.

It would appear in many cases that people become the weakest link for support. He was never surprised by the amount of care and love that most are not willing to give to people within the vulnerabilities of communities.

He personally attempted to make every effort to lift up their day with a smile and with words that came to mind as he related to his disability and their isolation.

Jimmy believed where happiness and joy may be challenged, God will be there to listen. He can be your best listener and push you through whatever the day brings so that maybe the promise of a better day tomorrow can be possible.

He strongly believed people are placed within everyone's life, and that can make the difference, if one paid attention, as visibility of His presence has to be found and accepted.

Many think it should be a great flash of light for all to see or it can't be real, but it can often be as small as a night-light for only you to see.

Jimmy had the opportunity to visit with others from around the world. People placed in his life from out of the blue, and he found we can make a difference, although we should let God do the rest.

Could it be any more exciting?

CHAPTER 12

Resolution

It was the ninth day of July 1997. Jimmy continued old work habits, leaving at six each morning and returning many times after his son was sound asleep. His long days that consumed daylight consumed the amount of time he would see his family during the daytime hours. Jimmy learned being the best dad is hard work and discovered the balance between providing for his family and being there for his family appeared to be unmanageable.

The large amounts of work and stress-related issues had taken over. His dedication to achieve success in all areas of his life was leaving the last step in question. Without delay, the climb became interrupted.

Jimmy had the endurance to withstand the hardships, although the limitations of his condition put him down for the fourth seizure of his lifetime.

Jimmy began a long series of testing over the next three months, and increasing his medication became necessary. Struggling with his marriage, Jimmy realized he would need to make some choices on the importance of family, his illness, and work. His life was running like the locomotive of a freight train.

The track seemed smooth with only a few bends, although Jimmy had discovered the passenger train may have been the better choice.

The skies remained blue but was filled with clouds in many shapes and sizes, although life was flashing outside the window without clear vision of anything passing by.

He needed to be home more, and his wife needed time to get out and revisit fun in her life. As soon as he was able, he began spending more time with his son doing hobbies. Dirt biking, basketball, baseball, and fishing became the shared activity whenever and wherever possible.

Jimmy's marriage had taken many wrong turns, and loneliness was shared by both.

Between his work schedule and his home schedule, it didn't leave a lot of room for imagination and companionship that would normally be within any marriage. The time needed to share love and bring happiness and joy, fulfilling the needs and wants and even desires for the other, had become remote. Their hands had become separated.

Love and happiness became challenged to the point where dreams became foggy, and accomplishments became unknown.

Jimmy had decided to seek counseling again and see if he and his wife would be able to work out their problems, although they separated in 1999 and divorced a year later.

Jimmy found himself unhappy once again—heartbroken, unhappy with his personal life and at work. His failures became more than a lesson. Fear of failing again became stronger than fear of survival. He continued making attempts to be the best dad he could and spent as much time with his son as possible. He also spent time in counseling, although the library of the many memories throughout his life became filled with regret and disappointment.

Years had slipped by, and four years later, Jimmy remarried. With every effort to retain his love for his new wife, her emotional and verbal abuse took its toll.

Jimmy placed great value on friendship, love, compassion, and honor and struggled with what was best for her rather than what was best for him. He had contacted a longtime friend that worked in the counseling field and asked her for some insight. He needed help understanding he was being abused again, although in a different way. He wanted to get away from this replay in his life.

Jimmy had a problem asking anyone for help, and it was difficult and came with emotional challenges. Yet it became obvious through verbalizing what was going on that he needed to take a break from the relationship. And that did not become hard to do.

As he was sitting having breakfast on a beautiful day at the ranch, his wife had informed him she had become involved with someone and indicated to Jimmy she was no longer in love with him and requested living in separate houses.

That was not a good path for Jimmy. Just days after, he walked away from this marriage. He realized the lack of love was so apparent. Jimmy had promised himself he would never allow another person to mistreat him ever again. This made this decision very easy.

This also brought up the many questions about his relationships and why he was unable to hold his together. He asked himself, *How can love between two people that have become best friends fail?* In his experiences, he had discovered that most people continue to love and, in some cases, continue to cherish the times they once shared together. He was one of those people. Lacking hate and actually embracing the happiness, the love, and the hope.

Dreams together seem to vanish, although a giving relationship can hold the memory, retain the wins, and move forward through the losses that contain the dreams.

Jimmy began thinking about how one person can be filled with happiness and love, although somehow, the other person will find loss in one or both emotional connections.

Can happiness and love survive without one another?

The dictionary tells us love is unselfish, loyal, having concern for the good of another, a warm attachment or enthusiasm, and devotion. Some people think love as simple, and others more serious.

Is love a word or a thought? Is it happy in the moment but lacking the commitment of carrying happiness and dreams into the future?

Experiences have given Jimmy better understanding of the dreams one could wish to accomplish and the importance to find love for ourselves and others.

It's fantastic. Love me, love others, and dream big!

Jimmy enjoyed being reminded of the beginning, the time when we are born and given the ability to love in abundance.

How do we lose the talent?

Maybe that's it. As friends, husbands, wives, partners, and parents, the need to pay attention to our children can hold the answer. Jimmy strongly believed if we honestly listen to our children, they remind us of the need for each other.

Jimmy taught his son to the best of his ability. He tried to teach him how to be a good person, never overlooking how he could show him by example how to help others, with examples of kindness and care.

We must always remember that adults have as much to learn from children as they learn from us. And, yes, we must not forget that early lessons can slip away, and happiness can easily lapse into the back of our memories.

Why is happiness not in the definition of love?

When Jimmy was born, he delivered real and untainted love, the kind of love gifted to everyone. It's delivered with a flash of light, to be carried to the end of time, and applied with unknown vulnerability. Jimmy discovered strength, although his flash had weakened.

Jimmy reminded his son each day he was loved, not just by him, but also by God. Faith to believe in goodness and kindness often becomes the forgotten lesson that is so important at a very early age. Jimmy believed clear and unconditional love becomes the need that fuels the energy of happiness.

The energy of happiness. That's something to think about.

No matter what spilled into his life, he always had the nudge to remember that he was loved and to stick with his hopes and dreams. At every opportunity, Jimmy always tried to tell youth they can be anybody they want to be. He also encouraged them to also do good things for others.

Jimmy had learned, as a first responder, way too many people believed they are not loved by anyone.

Ninety-nine percent of these people, no matter their race or religion, say they don't believe God loves them.

You can never get enough of what you

don't need to make you happy.

—Eric Hoffer

CHAPTER 13

Survivor

In 2014, Jimmy found the road he had traveled for so many years had become bumpy and unfamiliar territory again. His longtime career in floor covering and pounding nails took its last swing.

The pursuit of achievement comes with a cost, and Jimmy felt he had paid that price more than once. Often he was told he was hard to keep up with, that he rarely slowed down. His energy and drive to achieve his dream over the last twenty-eight years was all too familiar for him.

Jimmy's second wife once said he was the hardest working poor man she knew, although she wasn't paying attention. His streets may have been dirt rather than gold, and choices in business can vary in size, although in many ways, Jimmy felt he was one of the richest men alive.

It was true. Jimmy did work hard and often found himself working hard for the achievement of others. There is no greater feeling than when you are out in front, and you turn around to help others achieve things they had no idea of the possibilities.

Jimmy had become trapped in his own self. Stuck in time. Stuck where he was unable to accomplish true honesty within himself. Although the happiness he felt appeared genuine, it was a mirage floating above the surface of the sand.

It was where the warm sand became the thirst, and the body of water in the distance had become visible happiness. Reaching its destination continued to change, and yet he found himself standing in the middle of the desert, looking in every direction. He had learned that if he took time to be unhappy, travel those footsteps, cry just a little, then maybe the inspiration of truly being happy would give him all the water he desired. Jimmy was discovering that being happy with himself enlarged his knowledge of doing good things for others and intensified the love and joy for life.

It was day one of Jimmy's new job as a project manager for the remodeling of kitchens with a nationwide company. The projects were cabinets, drywall, and doors that filled the metal box that blocked the driveway. Two-by-fours and dust consumed the room that was once called the kitchen. Electrical wiring and plumbing became the enemy as the refrigerator became that new piece of furniture in the living room.

Welcome to stress, unhappiness, and being overwhelmed by the thought of having toast and orange juice on the couch. Jimmy enjoyed the opportunity to work with people that, in most cases, hadn't been sleeping well and couldn't wait to have their kitchen back.

Jimmy was very good at his job, and in most cases, he could literally see the kitchen in his mind as he worked through the many components of completion.

After a week had passed and Jimmy was settled in, he began reviewing projects unknowing to him as his managers were working up the details of eighty kitchens at a time.

Jimmy was told he would have about forty kitchens to start, and although that still seemed very unmanageable, Jimmy said nothing at the time and felt he could handle the challenge.

The following week, Jimmy was invited to the conference room for a team meeting. In the meeting, Jimmy sat quietly while he learned the culture, conversations, and format. As Jimmy listened carefully, the words and numbers of about five million in losses came up.

Jimmy's attention became more intense as he reviewed documents where losses seemed strange.

He was new at the table and didn't want to create a shock factor right off the bat, so he continued to listen and learn more about each member in the room.

The very long table was surrounded by many black high-back chairs and the pressure for Jimmy to become actively involved in the conversation wasn't completely necessary. Jimmy's director did look his direction, a little anxious to hear his thoughts.

The pages were legal size financial documents showing income and losses. Jimmy reviewed the categories as quickly as possible and wanted to be sure before he spoke.

He couldn't stand it any longer, and he shuffled in his high-back chair and decided to speak up.

"Could I please, I mean, can I say something?"

The directors in the meeting approved, and he began to speak, "We can change this."

Jimmy meant no disrespect. Although he was new, he just thought maybe he could help.

He hesitated for a second as the room became overly still, and it became clear why he was the first person hired from outside the family-operated business. Then Jimmy heard the words from another team member.

"I know you're new here and not with the program, although I have to tell you, we're here to lose money and make the floor covering division of the business more profitable."

The silence in the room became awkward, pens were laid across notepads, and Jimmy noticed the majority had become uncomfortably restless. It appeared the person sharing the information may have spoken about a shared secret within the family. The directors looked undecided as to move forward or move to another topic.

Jimmy quickly broke the silence after underlining various items within the profit and loss statement. It contained many pages without profit, and he began sliding them across and down the table. When everyone had a page and was able to identify the items Jimmy referred to, he passed around the page that clearly showed over a three-million-dollar win.

Now for some people, this most likely appeared as a division that was without profit. The problem was the building capital or the money to build the project had 40% floating in midair. Although without a calculator and digging in above Jimmy's pay grade, it would remain a mystery. Although stunned, he had worked through awkward conversations in the past and immediately responded, "We don't have to lose this much money, and if you think the owners of the company want to lose this much money, you're wrong."

Jimmy recognized the faces thinking it was impossible and the faces expressing interest. Without words, this would become his best tool moving forward. It seemed simple; inspire team members with bonuses by the end of the year. It was within the employment compensation plan, although goals were never achieved.

Jimmy was unable to inspire 40%, although he was able to get everyone on the same page. Negative faces became positive, filled by the fight to be happy.

Thirty-eight percent profits were recognized throughout team members within the next ten months.

In less than one year, the kitchen division became the most profitable piece of the company. Team members began recognizing the fun and happiness that goes with making money on their projects rather than feeling defeated every day.

Jimmy had received an email from the national office recognizing him for the turnaround and national copied everyone in the building and the company.

This did not sit well with family members. Jimmy could hear the noise of excitement throughout the room of about twenty-five project managers after reading the email. Jimmy's boss quickly showed up at his desk within seconds with panic in her face, almost pale and eyes wide open as she asked him not to respond to the email. This seemed inappropriate. He thought a simple thank-you would have been nice and recognized something was terribly wrong.

Why wouldn't they celebrate this major accomplishment throughout the office?

Team members had worked so hard, struggling through the days, blending their lunch and work as emails and phones attempted to steal the success. Jimmy realized what they had done. They had taken the credit through their own email chain.

The executive branch had most likely removed others from the message and claimed the victory as their own. A company set up for the deflection of recognition from national had suddenly showed enormous growth.

The national company slowly began moving their people in and pushing the family out. Jimmy thought maybe national had become interested by the fact they could still profit even more money after purposely losing money. Within thirty days, he found himself surrounded by people trying to learn his secret. Jimmy recognized they had purposely replaced his whole team with tenure from the national company, including one married to a corporate attorney.

What had Jimmy stumbled across? Was everyone directed or trained to lose money?

Jimmy's secret was simple. Be approachable. Be a partner in their success rather than a commander. He shared these talents with others. All they had to do was pay attention. People like to win. When they go home at the end of every day a loser, it rolls over into their life. All he did was help other team members feel like winners and accept the losses as the lesson.

When Jimmy was promoted, it sent a message and another great opportunity not just for him but for everyone in the building.

Great job and well done!

Over the next few weeks, project managers continued to come by Jimmy's desk and congratulate him on the successful turnaround they had thought was impossible.

Jimmy took the opportunity to congratulate them. Their contribution to the success of the project could not go unnoticed.

After a short time, Jimmy could see and feel the resentment from leadership. He continued to inspire new ways of creating happy installation crews on the front lines. Jimmy recognized their talents and continually complemented their work. This type of project management was very new for Jimmy. He never actually had face-to-face contact with customers or the installers. Paying close attention to the comments made by both parties within projects required a unique management skill. Jimmy knew the secret to success would only be found through personal and team function happiness.

He discovered the company he was so excited about had a lot of very unhappy people.

The extra challenge for Jimmy was the family. As many know, family can be a bit dysfunctional at times, although that's okay, maybe even perfect. He believed every person functioned differently on purpose. Otherwise, where would the creativity, hopes, and dreams be stored? Where would love for another appear?

Jimmy met with the vice president, a national tenured executive. They discussed the possibility of employees receiving some type of bonus as promised within the job description and compensation plan. To Jimmy's knowledge, team members weren't receiving the promise without making the profit.

A company purposely losing money with no profits, amazing, no bonuses.

Jimmy was also interviewing for a new position within the company, although he had a gut feeling about the conversation and decided it wouldn't be a good fit.

He was well-liked, and his energy rubbed off. The general happiness within teams became noticeable, and the new bonus didn't hurt either.

It was on a Friday in July 2015 when Jimmy found himself struggling with some type of health issue, without knowing the day would again change his life once more.

The day started as Jimmy awoke, and the ability to get up from the surface of his bed was difficult. Even his focus became strained. Sometime overnight, he had become sick and would not be able attend the announcement of his promotion as a new director of project management.

Jimmy had gone to his favorite restaurant the night before and had their famous mushroom Swiss burger.

He wondered if some onion had touched or was in his food. He has had bad reactions to onions, and the way he was feeling seemed similar. But there were other symptoms that seemed odd.

Jimmy managed to take a shower, although the bounce in his step was missing, and he remained uncomfortable. He had called the office to explain he was not feeling well, but he wanted to wait a little while before bailing for the day.

His hopes seemed simple. Feel better after some rest and return on Monday. Jimmy rarely was sick and rarely missed work, but this time, something was really off.

After Jimmy packed his bag and went to the front desk to check out, he again questioned himself about the horrible way he was feeling and debated staying over for the weekend.

Jimmy decided he just needed to return home, crawl in bed. He could rest, and things would be fine.

But things began to change rapidly. Jimmy became very fatigued and still not feeling well, so he stopped at a wayside rest and slept for a while.

The sun was shining, and the day was very warm. Jimmy parked in the shade, rolled all his windows down. He opened the sunroof and made a place to sleep in the back of his truck. Jimmy noticed as he looked out the window the day was filled with blue sky and few clouds. It was beautiful. The odd feeling of sickness appeared to have the better part of him, and he was so hoping this would pass.

When Jimmy woke a couple of hours later, he continued to feel very sick, and the onion thing appeared not to be the problem. He returned to the highway, setting his cruise control, and continued the last part of his trip.

Nine miles down the highway, Jimmy woke to the sound of car horns.

Jimmy raised his head, only seeing the lines on the highway, and apparently had become unconscious.

His vehicle left the roadway at sixty-five miles an hour.

After traveling through the ditch about four or five hundred feet, Jimmy's vehicle became airborne over the southbound lanes of the highway. With a bounce and a roll, the car landed on its side.

As Jimmy's eyes began to open slightly, images came into partial focus, and he began to hear the sounds of voices.

"He's waking up."

Jimmy realized he was restrained with his neck in a collar, with a basket over his face. The last thing he remembered was his car on the road, and he had no idea how he had become injured and strapped down to a backboard. Jimmy continued attempting to focus, asking what happened.

Jimmy heard the sound of voices, and his eyes were still attempting to open as he heard what sounded like a helicopter, which was actually landing outside of a hospital.

A voice identified himself as a doctor and told Jimmy he was in a hospital emergency room because he had been in a car accident on a highway. Jimmy found himself struggling to comprehend what he was hearing, although he couldn't seem to stay awake. His eyes closed.

The sounds of voices became a dream. Real with emotions, although faint without clarity. As Jimmy began to be more alert, the sudden feeling of being trapped was within his focus. Jimmy was relieved knowing he didn't have a seizure, although he continued struggling to understand what was happening to him.

He began feeling anxious and out of control. Vulnerability set in, and he began to struggle as the people in the room began calling out, "He's combative."

The next thing Jimmy knew, people were lying on top of him to keep him from falling off the table. He himself struggled to calm down but without success. The doctor finally was able to do that after a few attempts. Jimmy took a deep breath and was thankful it was over. He did struggle to stay awake, but fear set in as he became aware he had a serious problem.

Then a doctor came back with results. He informed Jimmy of their findings within his spine and neck regions, and they removed his collar and allowed some room to move.

The doctors asked Jimmy if he remembered what happened.

He told them he pulled over to rest and then got back on the road. The next thing he knew, he awoke to the sounds of car horns on the highway before the lights went out.

Jimmy had noticed the nurse changed his IV more than once, and although with time he began feeling better, the mystery illness remained the question.

He did begin to feel better and began discussing his medications and his seizure disorder. He told the doctors and the state trooper in the room that he did not feel this was a seizure but remained worried about what was going on.

The doctor told Jimmy he had a concussion and would need to rest, although he needed to wake from time to time and see his neurologist on Monday. Jimmy, although still recovering, quickly recognized the judgments made when dealing with brain injury patients, and he became a little disappointed.

The doctors and nurses had treated him with care, and Jimmy felt comfortable being discharged and returning home. He made an appointment for that following Monday and reported the accident to his employer.

After giving Jimmy an EEG, the report indicated he was having a different type of seizure and would require another medication. Although he told the doctor he didn't have a seizure, she had the data to back up her diagnosis. Jimmy was ordered to start taking the new medication until he would see his neurologist. He continued to remain fatigued and was feeling poorly, although he did retrieve the medication and began taking it as prescribed.

Jimmy went back to work for his first day as the new director of project managers for the stores located in Wisconsin, Iowa, Nebraska, and South Dakota.

He continued feeling a little off, although he was hoping after seeing his neurologist, he would feel better about adding medication to his regimen.

Jimmy had some reorganization on his desk to complete and asked his boss about the move to his office, as it appeared a project manager was using it.

To his surprise, she said he would not be moving as it wasn't necessary and should continue working at his desk. That was a little frustrating, and Jimmy would be the only director without an office, and that seemed strange and made him uneasy.

Jimmy felt he had become a vital leader within the community of project management, and now he felt he was being singled out in front of the rest of the management team.

On the way home after the accident, Jimmy was looking out the window of his son's car. He began watching the world go by with every mile, lost in deep thought.

At times, Jimmy had said he hated his brain and looked at himself as less perfect.

Although Jimmy was smart, and confident with his looks, he also felt he had the talent to fulfill his dreams. Now he felt he was being outwardly judged by others that delivered a very unpleasant message. He sensed people treated him differently than others, even doctors.

He perceived those doctors had treated Jimmy differently as a person because he had a brain injury, that he was thought of as a person not working with a full deck.

Could it be that brain injuries are all the same and, for the most part, taken like a grain of salt?

When Jimmy went to see his doctor, and after discussing his accident and the new medication, she insisted Jimmy continue taking it as prescribed.

Slowly he became sick again, sharing something was wrong to his son and family. Jimmy had found research and began convincing himself it was a concussion, as symptoms can continue for a length of time. Yet something still remained odd. He rested as much as possible, crawling in bed just after dinner and not getting up for ten or eleven hours. He tried to remain positive and optimistic about his recovery. He wanted to get back to his normal way of life.

Yet he continued to find himself in unfamiliar territory, so his frustration started consuming his thoughts and the things he loved. Happiness became aloof.

Why is this happening. What is wrong with me?

As Jimmy laiy flat on his back, his eyes attempting to stay open, the ceiling appeared smooth with dirty edges.

Jimmy began talking to God, saying, "I know you're busy, but I need your help. What is wrong with me, and what do I need?"

Jimmy continued working hard and trying to teach his team how to identify strengths and weaknesses within construction crews. His goal was to teach them to understand the importance of successful on-site project leaders. Jimmy always wanted his team to be part of the solution. Completing projects with fewer complaints, on-time completions, and within the budget creates and inspires positive attitude between all parties involved in the project, not just the customer.

Jimmy's boss had called him to her office. She mentioned noticing him struggle a little. She asked him if he thought the director job was too demanding for him. Jimmy stood confused by her question after milestones of achievements were apparently not being noticed.

He quickly realized that for some reason, she was trying to get him to quit. Were the milestones threating the endgame?

This made absolutely zero sense, because he knew the job. He felt his people skills were very in tuned to the job.

Jimmy reassured her things were good and moving forward, although he was feeling tired. To his surprise, tears came without words, emotions came without warning.

He decided he should take a medical leave effective immediately before she took the opportunity to remove his status as project director. He had worked very hard for this position, and it was well deserved.

Jimmy made another appointment to see his doctor. He informed her of his medical leave from work because of his continuing struggles. Jimmy mentioned he was feeling similar to the day of his accident. Again, he was sent home.

Within days, Jimmy's condition worsened. There was lack of energy and the ability to function as his normal self. He knew something was terribly wrong and informed his son that he would like to go to the hospital emergency room.

Hopefully, he would find out what was going on with his condition.

As he climbed into the car, he began feeling some relief. A doctor at the emergency room might have an idea of the possibilities of what could be making him feel so poorly. All Jimmy wanted was for someone to check his condition and help him feel better. He felt he was falling asleep forever.

On arrival, Jimmy explained to the triage nurse he was feeling terribly ill and thought it might be his medication.

"Are you still taking the medication?"

Jimmy replied yes and that he had been taking it for some time with no improvement.

After waiting for what seemed a long time, he was moved to a room, examined, and tested for a possible brain bleed. The tests were completed, and they came back with good results, although Jimmy was prescribed more medications.

Then Jimmy noticed the blood cart being pushed into his room. He heard the nurse and doctor cancel it out loud. The lab tech questioned why.

Jimmy couldn't hear the response because she had pulled the cart back from the doorway to his room. Jimmy again recognized the unusual treatment given to a person with a brain injury, and he became disappointed when it came from another doctor. Jimmy didn't know what to think. He was feeling horrible and wanted to go back to bed.

The next day, Jimmy felt worse. He was frustrated with the doctor's evaluation. He called his sister for help.

He was going to beg someone or anyone to help find out why his condition was worsening and hopefully complete the lab work to confirm whether the medication was making him sick. It had been almost six weeks since the accident, and the lab work had not been completed. Why wouldn't someone let him know his records had been updated without lab work results?

Why won't they check my blood?

Jimmy's doctor would not be in until Monday although his hopes were that her nurse would have the ability to assist with his request and the lab work could be completed.

Jimmy was learning what it must be like to see the world from inside a fishbowl.

Looking out from a broken run-down body, he saw the sun shining bright, the blue sky painting a mural as green trees filled the backdrop, and the wind was blowing the fresh air.

After visiting with the nurse, it was apparent to her that he should see his doctor again, and she could better evaluate his condition the following Monday. His doctor would be in a meeting, but she would ask her to take a quick look and write the order for a blood draw to determine the levels of his medications.

He remained frustrated as the weekend seemed like too many days to wait, but he also had some optimism for any kind of resolution. Monday would have to work.

Jimmy, with a second brain injury, seemed to grasp the need to fight for his own survival, and he did have the determination to do everything he could to survive. He just couldn't understand why he was in hospitals, fighting for his life and not getting any help.

Why was the lack of interest to help Jimmy or at least using all possible and reasonable resources before concluding it was in Jimmy's imagination?

Jimmy had expressed the importance he felt of someone checking his medications and the failure to look at the possibility of admitting him to the hospital for further evaluation.

In Jimmy's experience, it appeared that most brain injury patients are misjudged, maybe even mistreated by most. It appeared anything to do with the brain makes you stupid or simpleminded.

Jimmy had learned in many cases that judgment and mistreatment should offer options. Although his experiences had led him to believe some head injuries can be very difficult to diagnose, all require extra care so as not to treat all the same. He believed the signs were very noticeable, and there is no excuse for doctors to lack the ability to identify and separate weaknesses within patient care.

As Jimmy continued the struggle throughout the weekend, his body began to tremble, his head and ears began to ring. Soon Jimmy felt like life was being drawn from his body.

Monday, September 14, 2015, fifty-seven days after Jimmy's accident, he returned to the doctor's office. He sat in a chair with his arms folded, his hands tightly tucked beneath his armpits, his body trembling, and his head ringing with the high-pitched sound like microphone feedback.

Once again, he became surprised at the quick conclusion of his condition.

The first question from his doctor, with a smile on her face, was what the problem was. Jimmy began by telling her he felt horrible and his head was ringing. Her smile became bigger, and she asked Jimmy if he was hearing voices, as she sat down in her chair.

Jimmy, although angered by her comment, responded with, "No, something is terribly wrong, and the severe ringing in the head had been there since last Friday." He repeated the same thing he had said before, "Something is horribly wrong with my medications. Please check my blood. Something is terribly wrong, and I can't go on like this any longer. Look at me. I'm sick and need your help. Can't you see?"

Jimmy's body was trembling with the fear that death appeared to be knocking on his doorstep. Voices in the room became slower in motion, and the helpless feeling began to strip away another layer in Jimmy's head. His eyes fluttered in confusion. His morning medication began to increase the intensity of the high-frequency sound in his ears. He was aware of the slur in his speech. His lips and tongue would not work together. Jimmy looked at the floor. He looked around the room. He felt defeated and ignored. He began to lose hope.

Lacking help from his doctor was apparent, and God himself was invisible. Jimmy's faith became challenged, or maybe even absent.

The doctor got up quickly. She seemed offended and sounded angry as she said, "If something's wrong with your medications, I'll eat crow."

And without another word, she left the room.

Jimmy again felt judged, mistreated, as a brain injury patient, and any condition mentioned by him would be treated like someone with no idea of reality.

The worst part was he really liked his doctor and relied on her care for him for over twenty years.

Jimmy just wanted a simple blood test which he had never received even after the accident and before being prescribed additional medications. It seemed to him that nobody was interested in locating the cause of his continuing decline.

Finally, a blood draw was completed. He went home and directly to bed, worried about the outcome.

If my eyes close, will they open? Will I see the freshness of a new day, the freshness of the sky or the sun? Will I breathe its fresh air?

Then Jimmy heard his phone ring. He remained still without movement. The room remained dark as the ring became distant. Then silence. The phone began to ring a second time. Jimmy cracked his eyes, but the darkness continued beneath his eyelids without sound.

Jimmy began to dream of the unknown and the fear of his path.

Without warning, his eyes opened sharply. He gasped for air as he heard the ring of his phone again. It was the nurse from the hospital. It was then he noticed he had missed calls. He called back the last one, and the panic in the voice brought sharp attention to his ear. Then he heard bad news.

"Your levels are dangerously toxic. Discontinue the medication immediately."

The therapeutic ranges are between ten and twenty, but Jimmy's levels were well above fifty. Sixty is an irretrievable pharmaceutical coma or, in simple terms, brain-dead. Jimmy had worked so hard to care for himself over the years, and now, after over a month of complaining about his medications, his fear had become real and most likely damaging.

He had just saved his own life. It wasn't over by any means. Not until blood draws for the rest of the week would ensure Jimmy's survival and medications levels were back within therapeutic levels.

Jimmy believed he should have been recalled to the hospital for admission, although he never heard from his doctor after the accident occurred.

His next appointment came with some discomfort for all parties involved with his care. Jimmy's little brother was saved at this very hospital, and his disappointment became overwhelming. He even expressed his concerns with patient relation services. As he left that day, he passed by the nurse who had given him the time of day, listening to him with compassion, and understanding and seeing the possibility of a problem. It became the nurse that God had put in Jimmy's path. This was the nurse that highly irritated his doctor.

Jimmy, with tears in his eyes, hugged the nurse, as he whispered in her ear, "Thank you for saving my life."

That was the last time Jimmy would see her. He was hoping and praying she would be recognized for her skill and for the compassion she had for her patients. Jimmy searched for her at his next appointment, checking the hallways, the nurses' stations, and lobby.

Then he saw her in a different department and felt relieved and grateful she wasn't wrongfully terminated for questioning a superior. Jimmy recognized her bravery and the courage it had to take as she stood against the doctors that had created the problem.

CHAPTER 14

Inspiration

Over the next few months, Jimmy took some necessary time to heal physically and mentally. His incredible opportunity to work with others would continue, teaching them to identify their strengths, achieve personal goals, and find happiness within their work. That was so important to him.

When Jimmy did return to work, he was greeted by friends. These other employees that, over time, had become important to him. They were the footings that remained strong, like walls that held their sturdy value, and its roof maintained the victory. Jimmy's day was fueled by seeing others return home each day feeling successful of their accomplishment.

The welcome back was filled with excitement, and with no surprise to them, Jimmy hit the floor running, just like he had never been gone. To Jimmy's surprise, the atmosphere in the office felt a little strange. He soon would discover the hard work accomplished by the many people had been dismantled.

Jimmy's team appeared stressed. There were many issues unresolved, workloads appeared overwhelming. He quickly asked, "What happened?"

Tension accompanied blank faces. Seconds passed without words. Looks at each other expressed disappointment as Jimmy asked, "Wasn't anyone helping you?"

To his surprise, the answer was no.

Jimmy immediately apologized to his team, and without notice, he found himself judged and mistreated by the company he dedicated himself to. One of his colleagues, the previous director before his promotion, seemed agitated. His movements appeared irregular, his walk was rapid and aroused attention throughout his team.

Then with a sudden stop at Jimmy's desk, he stated a question about an issue that needed to be resolved. Jimmy quickly responded with "no problem, I got it!"

The words Jimmy had no idea would ever be spoken became real, direct, and with intention.

"Are you sure, with your brain problem?"

Jimmy had worked twelve-hour days with no additional pay. He would turn the lights on when he would arrive and turned them off when he would leave. He inspired the others. Achievements that reduced losses within the thirty-two-million-dollar company lacked appreciation for his efforts.

"Think, Jimmy, just think. You got this."

The office was an open area with dividers. Jimmy felt the discomfort among other teams.

Each step came with additional discomfort, although he kept his head up as he always did. Compassionate faces filled the room.

As Jimmy entered the breakroom, he noticed the president of the company pouring himself some coffee. He quickly shook off the past and made conversation. They talked briefly about floor covering, and the president shared some of his history as a carpet installer and where he had started in the industry. Jimmy had also mentioned some of his history as a carpet installer and where he had started.

Jimmy was startled with his next words.

"Get out of here!"

Jimmy was standing behind him and thought maybe he heard him incorrectly and replied, "What?"

"I mean it. Get out of here."

Jimmy left the breakroom, and within minutes, his boss arrived at his desk. He thought they were going to the conference room, although she took him in to the human relations office just down the hall.

"Jimmy, please sit down."

The next words came with some surprise due to Jimmy's coverage area being one of the biggest territories in the company.

"We are eliminating your position as director."

Jimmy's vulnerability and the disappointment of no longer working with some great people put him in *that* territory again.

"It's okay. I'll be okay!"

Then the words that were like nails bending as they are driven in to wood came. He was told to collect his personal things from his desk and leave. He was also told to not talk with others on his way out.

The company that had no idea of its potential, or the level of profit possible, which became possible with Jimmy's help, eliminated his job.

Jimmy's ability to identify weakness and strengths within performance and learn from its experiences gave him the ability to apply the knowledge to their desires of performance. He helped the team's stretch to the achievements of their dreams.

He continues to believe the things we do for others becomes the pursuit, and the most rewarding and accomplished personal goal of most people are overlooked.

Jimmy was given those opportunities throughout life, and he rarely overlooked them as he grew as a person. The disappointment he felt was real and without words. The clouds began to gather, and the sky began to darken. His dreams of opportunity went into the fog that covered the ground, and uncharted footsteps became the route.

Jimmy began searching for inspiration. He was desperate for interpretation of what just happened. His mind was filled with whys, although gratefulness for life continued to be most important.

Jimmy's opportunity would be remembered as one of his greatest accomplishments. It was a time where people recognized the battle isn't with what you want; it's about where you want to go and how you want to get there.

The inspiration is not what you do alone; it's discovering what you can do together.

Jimmy's life, although filled with turmoil, completed who he is as a person, and how he had learned to love and cherish happiness as love itself.

In September 2015, it had been six weeks after Jimmy's accident, leaving him with yet another brain injury. This time it would be different for Jimmy. Although unintentional, it appeared Jimmy was having difficulty from toxic levels of pharmaceuticals, and even after many tests, the symptoms Jimmy experienced continued to be challenging.

Walking remained difficult and painful; running appeared to be impossible. Still, Jimmy remained positive and continued to fight against the inevitable. He continued to give the hospital an opportunity to determine how to better help with his care or at least be truthful of their intentions.

His inspiration for tomorrow is how he can make someone's day a better day, a day filled with a blue sky and nights filled with bright stars.

The damage caused by mistakes appear to attack Jimmy each day. It shows its ugly face of weakness and pain as the ringing in his ears remains the reminder of the accident that almost took his life.

Jimmy shuffled his way through the days, hoping to capture happiness as his savior and constantly reminding himself of all life's treasures.

It is said that trauma can recapture memories. Jimmy holds his family tightly to his heart, and the loves in his life, where the opportunities to create happiness and love beyond his greatest dreams will remain closely held as treasures in his lifetime.

Jimmy still has the slalom ski wrapped in plastic as a reminder he was one of the best water skiers in the country.

He's reminded continually with enormous amounts of God's love for him, where measurements are found in inches, feet, yards, and miles. Where the disappointments seem further away as he cherishes imperfection rather than death.

Now disappointments make his life full, as without them, life has no lessons.

Jimmy truly believes the knowledge of God's love for his people throughout the world is known by many and has no boundaries, no colors, and no religion.

It's pure, simple, and full of strength in love and happiness, and available for everyone and anyone that wants it.

As Jimmy recaptures his sea, its waters are blue and as far as he can see, a flood of love, the body of hope, and the happiness he was born with. This inspires reason to continue across its waters.

Jimmy had asked his doctors to please recognize when someone is reaching out for help, because in some cases, brain injury patients might just be right about what they are feeling, and it never hurts to look. He did receive a new doctor, but without the traditional letter a patient receives when a doctor is leaving the practice.

Jimmy sat alone at times, isolated and withdrawn, removing himself as hidden pain and struggle can be overwhelming.

Unemployed for the first time in his life since graduation, he decided it was time to take a road trip across the country.

Inspiration had come from when Jimmy was a little boy. He wondered how life would regain function, how emotions and passion would get back on track within life's journey. Where major events in one's life seem to change who he becomes as a person, the unknown had become interesting, and, yes, with challenges. Its discovery became exciting, and maybe it would introduce Jimmy to the time needed away from his normally busy schedule and be beneficial to his recharge.

Jimmy finds in many cases that people with injuries, missing limbs in wheelchairs, dying from cancer and other diseases, appear to be more positive people than people with everything they ever want or need to be happy.

Life appears to have new value when it's stripped away.

Jimmy learned that when death comes near, we discover, sometimes, the things we thought important become small and the things we throw away as junk each day, or each month, or even each year, are really the things we truly need.

Attention to the junk—can it be that simple?

Jimmy always spent most of his time on achieving his dreams, swaying away from the fear of rejection.

In turn, he thought he avoided the dwelling on factor and found comfort and more happiness this way. Jimmy had found unselfish love was better, and being loyal to himself could bring happiness. Concern for the good of another leads to victory. Enthusiasm and devotion to himself and others brings happiness, love, and joy to each day.

It appears Jimmy had found most of the answers he desired, and although he stands with many, it only appeared he stands alone. He always reached to the furthest causes. He found caring for others brings enormous joy and happiness, yet the feelings become real and different every time.

The well-being of all people around the world that hide behind walls because of their difference, being unacceptable, or being challenged with injuries or disease, will always remain as unfinished business that was created by unwanted circumstances.

As Jimmy drove throughout the days, he found it quite amazing. He found himself thinking about the concrete beneath his rubber tires, the people that paint the strips down miles of roadway, and, of course, the amount of gas his vehicle was consuming as he passed each mile marker.

Jimmy noticed the things in his life that consumed his time and energy seemed to disappear as he drove. It wasn't until later that he realized what it was. Time alone, time without responsibility, and most importantly, just being proud of the person he had become.

When Jimmy finally decided to return home from the trip that really didn't have an end date, he felt stronger and was thankful to himself for taking the time away. Soon the wheels of his truck would be reintroduced to his driveway.

When Jimmy did get home, he found a job offer on the table. It looked like he would be able to continue working within his field of low-income housing. The job would give him the opportunity to continue to work with the people that have very little but were filled with hopes and dreams just like everyone else. Another place where Jimmy could share happiness and inspire joy with people he knew well and people he didn't know at all.

The road trip gave Jimmy the time he needed to be reminded of unlimited love and hope for new dreams.

Dreams filled with mysteries.

Lacking regrets where life is filled with bright lights and dark rooms as they coexist. Jimmy will always share his belief with others.

Things can be better.

Jimmy will always remain with an open mind, and his ability to learn every day until his last, because "things are good enough," only holds back the happiness all deserve.

In 2019, Jimmy had decided to have the most challenging conversation of his life. Fifty years later and way too long, but he wanted to finally apologize to his little brother for his lack of protection on the night he was almost killed.

With tears in his eyes, he had to talk about that night so long ago. Jimmy started to speak, even though his little brother told him he needed to let it go. The conversation turned uncomfortable between them, but he wanted his little brother to hear his words of apology.

CHAPTER 15

Love's Greatest Challenge

Jimmy's little brother had very little idea how the night that almost took his life permanently attached itself within Jimmy's mind. The imprint remained. Tall like a building, unable to see its rooftop, fearing its fall, as the windows reflected uncertainty. He always thought they would talk before now, but he never was quite strong enough.

After Jimmy's brain injury, somehow the words became lost, although never forgotten. His life then became consumed by his own problems. The load of guilt and shame of that night remained hidden for another time.

As one of Jimmy's best-kept secrets was placed in the shoebox on the top shelf in the closet, the memory, although covered in dust, suggested it was time to throw it away. Jimmy had discovered later in life that if his little brother had not survived, he probably wouldn't have survived either. The loss would be greater than anyone had known.

Jimmy questioned unfairness and cruelty in the world at times. Faith can be challenged. Cursing God's name can be the distraction.

Many questions remain unanswered. The anger covers the moment as hurt drips from one's eyes.

Jimmy feels all people are given a gift at conception. Love and happiness are in abundance, and the adventure called life should be full of hope, security, and excitement.

Jimmy's pursuit to find answers to both fairness and, yes, cruelty in the world continued as a challenge. He reminded himself of the place where the groundwork of opportunity remains very real, a place where hope lines its walls and dreams covers its floors and happiness is held first and fear is ignored.

Jimmy learned each day brings new beginnings, rolling, turning, and splashing new energy. A rose garden might not bring bright colors and the smells of fresh beautiful soft petals each day, but there was the possibility of happiness, love, and joy for him, if he wanted it.

Life can always have unfair consequences, and loss of the people most precious to us can contaminate one's faith.

Jimmy believes it's not God's will; it's life.

Jimmy found that the changes in everyday life come with two different meanings. There is the acceptance of something different, accompanied by anger, or it can be the encouragement needed for the promising new day.

As Jimmy was given great opportunities from time to time, he tried to share the encouragement with the people around him.

Jimmy learned. You go out and get it. You fight for it and never give up. His hope and happiness demanded it. Achieving his dreams required it. He needed to squash the stories that were bringing him down; eliminate the self-pity and complaints of pain, because he was not alone. Someone somewhere has the same story. Jimmy avoided the negative "it doesn't get any better."

Because he knew he could always do better, always be better—not perfect, just better.

Today Jimmy continues to stand strong and hopes his story will possibly inspire you to take the time, pull the shoebox, dust its cover, and look at things you can do without. Jimmy learned secrets he held so close. Those that interfered with his happiness, the love and healing he needed for the very strength of his soul.

Jimmy has so much love to give to others, but he continues to be challenged by the thought of giving away the same happiness and love he needs for him. It isn't that everyone needed to know everything to be happy.

Jimmy never lost sight of the things he found the most exciting even as a little baby, but he found living the fine line where the balance of hurt, good, and the great questioned his own worthiness for love and happiness.

He found the hurt fights against the good, the good fights against the hurt, and where the great becomes weakened as the negative controls the outcome.

Jimmy learned that although people hear and learn about self-worth, the question remains: why is deserving of love and happiness for oneself held outside or second?

There are times when many find themselves filled with everything life has to offer, then question if it's okay to be happy and loved by another.

Jimmy found forgiving himself was powerful all by itself. Of course, he had to learn it the hard way over a lifetime of fear of rejection, the fear of anyone wanting to love him with his condition. He soon collected all the good and began doing what God had intended for him all along. Move forward with determination, knowing times will continue to be challenging, and have the courage to face the unknown and believe in his future.

Believe. What an incredible word of personal power and strength!

He began to rebuild as he was reminded of the love and kindness he received from his mother before he entered the world. The fresh water washing over the bumps and curves of his body, smoothing and polishing before he was wrapped in a warm blanket and placed in his mother's arms. A new world of uncertainty as Jimmy found himself filled with mystery and excitement.

Jimmy always knew his injury would eventually catch up to him with age, although his second brain injury wasn't in the plan. It will most likely shorten his quality of life a little sooner. These types of injuries can continue to grow like unwanted weeds in the garden. He has been given the opportunity to fight the weeds and plant a few roses. You know the kind with beautiful, bright colors and soft petals. But his strength now comes from his family, his friends, and the people around him.

The transition through the good, the bad, and the ugly helped Jimmy find the tools he had searched for over the years. He had no idea that relationships for him would be complicated with failures or self-destruction.

Sometimes finding the answers to questions can be very hurtful. But fortunately, letting the world in can also be as exciting as taking your first steps on earth!

Jimmy enjoyed watching as his son took his first steps. One foot reached for the next with unstable balance and then the fall.

Notice the next time you see a baby take those first steps. Watch their face as they learn not just how to walk, but how they begin to explore their life's journey. How quickly they become interested in learning and getting to where they want to go.

Jimmy remembers when his son would get to where he was going. He would turn around with a smile on his face, filled with happiness and the pride of his accomplishment. Jimmy's happiness with life comes from the people within it.

Where many people think about the impossibilities of a brain injury patient, he is a reminder that anything is possible. For some, it might take longer. It might come with frustration and maybe even some disappointment. With one foot in front of the other, focusing less on the short journey and more on the long will generally get one there every time.

Jimmy has discovered as he continues to grow as a person, the disability isn't the problem. Race or religion isn't the problem. Giving up on yourself and God's love, that's the problem.

Love for one's self is enough. Just don't let anyone or anything take it away!

With daylight, with its blue sky and clouds changing their shape and the night sky with its darkness bringing the sparkle of stars and the moon moving throughout time, we are constantly reminded of change.

Jimmy trusts that if we teach our children well, change will allow everyone everywhere to know they matter. Their dreams can be anything their heart sets out to accomplish.

In Jimmy's case, he hit the floor more than once. If it happens to you, you might hit it hard also, but you need to get up and move on, or at least make the effort, and have no regrets.

The challenge of judgment and the mistreatment of others will most likely remain throughout time. Many people in Jimmy's world have very little idea of the awareness he has because of his injuries.

As brain injury continues its journey through the medical world, there will still be fragments of misunderstanding, judgment, and even lack of compassion. It is a difficult field. Even when the vulnerable determine to move forward, it's not without a challenge.

Without Jimmy's knowledge at the time, he believes he chose a career where he saw life's challenges were witnessed in everyday life. Where the old become weak and die, our disabled or injured live in isolation, and our poor become trapped in the cycle of low income or no income.

Jimmy saw places where dreams became forgotten, or even unknown. Life becomes the struggle, inspiration becomes the challenge, and walls become the only security someone knows.

Jimmy's forty-year journey has given him the opportunity to help create programs. With computer labs and teachers to help navigate through daily struggles and churches with pastors to help inspire hope and where faith can emerge.

Low-income housing holds the hopes and dreams of people within its walls. Learning can become the dictionary of joy and happiness.

It's now the year of 2021, and although you can't see him, he stands beside you. You are not alone, and you are not unnoticed.

Be strong, stay special, and Jimmy encourages you to recognize what makes you happy and find the way to make your dreams come true. Even Jimmy found that sometimes what we see with our eyes and minds can overpower what we see or feel with our hearts.

Where faith is challenged by its design. Ugly, hurtful, and maybe unbelievable at times, faith can actually become the strength to carry us through. Although Jimmy understands it can lack inspiration in some moments, the hope doesn't totally vanish, and recognizing the love becomes the encouragement.

Jimmy wants others to cling to any love we are given, because love, although sometimes deeply hidden like treasure, can be found on another day.

Many say faith is only religious beliefs, and believing in something where there is no tangible proof is ridiculous, and that believing and trusting in a God should always raise questions. Jimmy is a believer and strongly believes if faith is not challenged, it carries no weight. It has no power.

Some question, If faith is to be true, then why does God save some and not others? Jimmy has wondered the same thing many times.

Life is to be born, a time to learn, love, and be grateful.

As we move through life, we discover the very essence or special qualities of vulnerability. Yes, vulnerability, and it doesn't make us weak.

Faith can be found in love and its lessons. Its truth is not what we see with our eyes. It's the feeling found within the love in our hearts. It's the love placed within everyone. Circumstance is unable to break it. Pain, the change and its aftermath, attempt to discourage our challenges, although faith holds it together.

As Jimmy sits on the front steps these days or looks out the window at the world, he recognizes the love. He recognizes the power of faith, and he is reminded of the wealth placed within him in the beginning.

The mounds of his life have been lifted. The layers have been separated and cleaned. His edges smoothed and polished. He finds himself ready for the journey of tomorrow.

The world continues to turn, and its wealth cradles love. As judgments form our choices, the hands of our children hold us together. When people all over the world learn that first step, that first adventure across the room, the smell of fresh air, the touch of a fresh flower, we experience love of who we are or who we believe we should be.

In Jimmy's story and many others, love will carry challenges. Love comes in many different forms.

The writing place on the wall of personality becomes each individual definition. Holding its own story, displaying its own victory, and carrying its own beauty.

In our world today, we speak different languages. We look different, and our cultures are shaped differently through personal and/or religious beliefs. We live with disabilities, other than physical.

Our love and kindness can look very much the same. Jimmy believes the love for one another was the intention of humanity, and we were never meant to hate. Somehow, because of our differences, abuse of each other, verbally, physically, and mentally, has become the natural way of order.

Do you believe in the love and kindness you were given in the beginning?

When you felt the touch of your mother's hand on her tummy as she tried to comfort or calm you, do you ever wonder if you touched back or wiggled your toes or smiled as she spoke with soft words of love and happiness for your future?

Did you kick with excitement?

Jimmy believes you were perfect when you entered this world. You are loved and gifted as perfect. Whether you are unable to see or speak, God knows you are there and you will not be forgotten and you will never be alone, as his wealth has been placed within you.

Love's greatest challenge is simply the lack of the word *happiness* in its definition.

The End

Happiness is love. You don't need it, you
don't want it, because you already have it.

—Todd Saucier

ABOUT THE AUTHOR

 Todd Saucier is not a pastor or minister, and he is not a doctor, nor is it his intention to push religion or give medical advice. Todd is a survivor of a brain injury and became inspired to share a story of strength and courage filled by endurance to achieve and accomplish lifelong dreams.

Someone who lived the life of judgment and mistreatment, where those who knew of his injury used it against him as he was tormented and treated with very little respect as a person.

Todd wanted to write this book as a reminder that unwanted circumstance can be invisible, and what's visible always has a story. Approximately 1.4 million brain injuries happen each year, and one billion people struggle worldwide. We are not alone, although we tend to live life in isolation, hiding from visibility.

If you are with a disability or injury of any kind and have read or about to read this story, please know it comes to you with love and understanding, not just by Todd and Jimmy but by God.

Where diversity around the world tends to divide us, injury or children born with challenge reminds us we are very much alike.

Thank you for your interest in his book, and remember to hug the happiness, hold the love, and always remember today is new, like fresh flowers with bright colors.

Just don't forget the attention and care!

CPSIA information can be obtained
at www.ICGtesting.com
Printed in the USA
BVHW08205908122
651441BV00008B/250